I'M THAT GIRL

Megan Anne Gallagher

Vanessa~
I'm so happy to
have met you!
Looking forward to
our adventures
ahead!
Megan

I'm That Girl

Megan Anne Gallagher

Edited by D.C. Santos

Artwork by Elisabeth Hannah Ammann

Photography by Leigh Marie Photography

ISBN-13: 978-1456588090
ISBN-10: 1456588095

For more information, please visit
www.magallagher.com

**It is strongly recommended
that a parent or adult guardian
decide whether this material is appropriate
for readers under 17 years of age.**

This is dedicated to the little kid in all of us.
Remember to love him/her endlessly; selflessly.

And to the most beautiful flower girl in the whole
world...Anna Gallagher

Special thanks to my Lioness of God, for loving
me immediately and unconditionally. And also,
to my very special Jedi, for being patient with me
(even when he doesn't want to be) and for loving
me because of it all, as opposed to in spite of it all.
Thank you Universe for allowing me to find the
strength and courage to write these truths.

And to Victoria Lampert ~ the mother, the angel,
the friend, the wisdom bearer ~
and one of the first people that told me that my job
on this planet was to write this book.

NAMASTE~~ (I bow to you; we are One)

3

The basis of the human experience
is to be in constant pursuit of something.

--*The woodland philosopher, Michael C. Lewis*

CONTENTS

INTRODUCTION

I spent a good chunk of my 20's addicted to some pretty awful things and behaviors. Much less than sober most of the time, I graduated college Summa Cum Laude, but my lifestyle still kept me away from myself. This meant that I wasn't writing for myself, only papers for school. When I started the whole divorce process, and started reconnecting with myself, I started writing again. My therapist, a fellow author, and I did a TON of cathartic writing, which is the basis for this book. In my mind, cathartic writing is an unfiltered, uncontrolled, and totally raw release of emotions. I write things that I would not write, or even think, at any other time. The language is harsh and the tone is often ugly. The words and images may appear mean and nasty with intent to cause pain. But that's not the goal of this type of writing, at least not for me. It is literally an attempt to purge myself of the emotional toxins, all of them. It is releasing all of the ugliness onto a page, like the verbal vomiting of poisons that inflict pain and discomfort. I truly wish no ill-will or harm to anyone mentioned on these pages. I am sure there will be some readers that don't believe me and think this is just an egocentric attempt to air my dirty laundry, but those readers would be very wrong.

So anyway, all I really have left to do now is this beginning and the end, but it's hard for me and I'm not really sure why. I'm struggling with it. I'm kind of resistant to it, which means there's some serious material in here that I am not ready to look at. So I guess, even while I thought the majority of the cathartic writing was done, there is still more to go.

The reason why this is difficult to put in words is: there is no real start or ending. It is a perpetual, never-ending journey. As mine differs from yours, yours is different from hers, and her's is different from his, yet they are still all intertwined, interlaced, and interconnected in a way that creates this amazing tapestry called existence. UGH. Every time I try to begin this, it comes out forced and muddled and not really saying what I mean to say. So I think the best thing for me to do is to just talk and to write. Let it come out as it will, naturally. To simply open my access to the Voice and let it speak through my fingers. After all, that's how all of my best writing occurs anyway. When I shut up and let HIM do the talking.

So, who is this "him"? What is this "voice"? HEAVY SIGH. This is where it becomes so much more complicated. This is not just telling a story. This is explaining something that has no words, but instead is made of sound, shape and feeling. It is a language all unto itself. It is EVERYONE'S native language, before the talking-kind begins. It is the language that lives within all of us, the voice that breathes life into our body, love into our hearts, and wisdom into our souls. It is beautiful, it is graceful, and it is perfect. It is the language of children. Think about a child that is having difficulty verbally expressing his emotions. He can, most likely, act or play it out - to demonstrate a reality that in some way does not involve words. This is because it is a matter of translating from this "wordless" language into the confines of our social constructs, AKA words.

Perhaps if I can describe my own experiences with this language, with this Voice, it will make more sense. My Voice sits way back in the left side of my brain. I can almost feel it in there. When all is quiet and I am seeking the answers that lie within my cellular memory, the knowledge and memories that accumulate lifetime after lifetime, my awareness brings me to that spot. The voice that comes out of my mouth when I speak from that place is different. It is deeper. It is calmer. There is a strength and confidence that is different from my normal, everyday presence. While I call this a "Voice", it's really not. I do not hear words come from this place. I do not even really hear sounds. I feel vibrations and it is these vibrations that provide me with the information I need. When I say that I can "read energy", I mean that I can feel the vibrations that roll off of people. I can feel it from five feet away. The natural language of the universe, the language of love, has no words. There are no discernable sounds. There are just feelings...and a feeling is nothing more than a vibration. Think about when someone asks you to describe how you FEEL, or what emotion X (happiness, sadness, excitement, etc.) FEELS like. You may relate it to an event, but you can't really describe it. It is not possible to truly describe feelings within the constraints of words. We stumble and stammer, trying so hard to get it out. Why do you think there are so many greeting cards? It is because it is nearly impossible to describe with words what we FEEL. The harder we try to explain it, the farther away from raw feeling we get. This is why music is so often used as a backdrop to set a mood, a tone, or a FEELING. Sound is so very important to our experiences, but it's not really sound. It is vibrations. Even those that cannot hear can FEEL the vibrations of music. They can move to the beat and be swept up with raw emotion because the beat is a vibration and a vibration is a feeling. You can't describe a vibration with words, so what makes us think it is possible to describe a feeling with words? It isn't...

So this part of the story is my feeble attempt to use words to explain the organic truths that live in my Voice. These truths have come to me after many, many lifetimes. I have been male. I have been female. I have been a kind person. I have been a murderer. I have killed and I have saved. I have lived. I have sat on all points of the pendulum that is our social morals, and I have seen many differing perspectives. Perhaps it is as a result of this broad range of experiences that I have been given the task of sharing this knowledge. I am not alone in this work. I am not the first nor will I be the last. But I am one that may be heard by those that can hear no others, because I will do my very best to use words that resonate with the natural voice; that speak using our native tongue of vibration. This is not an attempt to show you how much I know. This is an attempt to be the vessel to carry down the words of God, the words of the Goddess, the words of all beings larger than us, and to join them together once again. For only united will we find harmony and peace.

I will break this down into topics and will do my best to stay on topic. Tapping into ancient archetypes is not an exact science. They will simply be in the order that they are re-revealed to me. These are not my words. These are a gift from the unseen Masters. I take pride in being their medium, but I do not take credit for these thoughts. I am nothing but a messenger. Please remember, retransmitted sound turns to jumble. By this I mean that the messages are handed down to me in sounds and images, not words. So I'm basically translating these into the English language. And translations are not always 100% perfect. This is the introduction to my story. Hopefully when you're done with these pages, you'll understand the messages that I'm trying to convey.

LOVE

Love is the center of the universe. It is the cosmic, psychic, spiritual glue that holds it all together. There is nothing more powerful than love, nothing more fulfilling than love, nothing more desirable than love. The problem is that people need it so badly that they are frequently willing to go to any length to get it. Another problem is that it can be falsely achieved through things that are less-than-healthy. Drugs are a perfect example. When one starts using drugs, the people in his/her inner drug-circle become his/her best friends, his/her closest confidants, his/her family. But in a moment of truth and redemption, these people will rarely, if ever, be there through thick and thin. It is just the worship of false idols. Any time we substitute pure love with something else, even if it seems to be real, we are worshipping a false idol. It is not that God wants us to worship only Him. It's that God wants us to be in a place of pure love always. ALWAYS. There are a million substitutes for it, all of which offer the appearance of being real and substantial. But they are not. Love is the only thing that's real, it is the only thing that God wants for us, and it is the only thing that matters.

Please note that whenever the term "God" is used, I mean it as an encompassing term that covers all beings of worship that represent love in the universe, regardless of the actual religion.

When it all comes down to it, "God" is the representation of life and all of its joys and struggles to regain oneness with love in the most pure sense of the word.

DEATH

Death is not the end. It's not even the beginning. It's simply a change. It's a move from one vehicle and one plane to the next. The sadness we feel after a loved one dies is based on earth-bound rules and selfish motivation. It's our inability to deal with change. The dead are not gone. They have not left us. Their energy has forever become merged with our own. We are eternally fused with those we love, even after death. That bond is carried forever and was created long before what we call time. It's a bond that has been with us forever. We are never really alone. We tend to travel with the same sets of energy from one life to the next. We don't always move together, but we always find one another. We always have family. We always have love, and death cannot stop that. Death is really like the taxi waiting to take us to our next destination. Sure, we miss those that have left us, but because of love, we can feel confident that we will see them and realign our energies again.

VOICES

There is a huge difference between the real Voice and the voices we are programmed with.

The real Voice, at least in my head, sounds like me. It is the Voice that I've been trained to ignore by the people that inflicted me with the other voices. These other voices are wrong, bad, mean, and earth-bound. They are shallow in comparison. They do not speak the truth, because they know the truth will banish them. They are generally much louder than the other Voice and much easier to listen to, because we are literally trained to do so. By our family, society, the media...By everything physically around us. However, if one listens to the global, collective, and utterly amazing song of the universe, we get to hear the truth. The Voice is the sound that snow makes as it falls; the sound of the wind rushing through the falling leaves; the sound of the blazing sun on a sweltering August day. That is the true Voice of reason and reality. The rest is just bullshit. The programmed voices are like little Gremlins put in our path to keep us from succeeding. Because if we succeed in our life's journey and reach levels higher than the people in our lives (the people that have programmed us with the bad voices), what does that mean for them? It means that if they also aspire to change, then THEY must take a hard look at themselves and see where their flaws lie. It means THEY were wrong, are wrong, and will continue to be wrong. Those are the fucking voices of hell itself. They are the voices that beg us to fail so that we will not leave and rise to the next level. In doing

so, we leave them cold and alone to wallow in their selfish pity and foolish pretense.
~~~~~~~~~~~~~~~~~~~~~~~~~~~~~~~~~~~~~

I understand the huge risk I am taking by writing these words. Many of my secrets will be grossly exposed. My life will literally be an open book. I will be scrutinized, criticized, disowned, hated, and become the outcast I've so often felt that I am. I am terrified to know what people will think of me. I will be perceived as arrogant. As thoughtless. As careless. As stupid. And even as I write this, I feel sick to my stomach. I can so easily share my story and my truth with people on a piece-by-piece basis through a very careful selection process. So, instead of keeping up the happy facade, I choose to fall from grace. To the people who think that they know me: here it is, all out in the open. Realize that you only know whom I show you. Hopefully you will begin to understand in turn that the people who know you only know the part of you which you want to be seen. We are all constructed of many, many layers. It is not my job to pull apart your layers and examine them, just as it is not your job to pull apart my layers. Yet, here I am, giving you each of my layers on a platter. Why? Why am I doing this? It's quite simple. The message is almost painfully simple: We do not have to continue to live by the messages we have been programmed by. We all have our own choices and we can live the life we want. It is our choices that define us.

17

Obviously, when we are little and our only sphere of influence is the adults in our life, we have no choice. Or rather, we have limited choices. But hopefully there comes a time in every adult's life where he/she stops, sits down, and evaluates. He/she reflects on the past, looks hard at the present, and visualizes the future. And if there are inconsistencies where he/she is today and where he/she wants to be tomorrow, it should be clear that change must happen and that the only one able to make the change is oneself. **Nobody else can do it for you**.

~~~~~~~~~~~~~~~~~~~~~~~~~~~~~~~~~~

The purpose of sharing these stories is to illustrate the messages that determined my choices for many, many years. It is to show how I eventually learned that I was living by someone else's rules. Some of the stories are really short and some are very long. Some of the philosophical stuff is more long-winded than others. This whole process started as the cathartic writing exercise (which lasted about five years and is explained earlier) in an attempt to release the poison that has haunted me my entire life. I'm now 37 and with a man whom adores me. He has reaped the benefits of this verbal exorcising of my demons. I would have been ill equipped for this relationship had I continued to hold onto all of this. While there is (and quite possibly will always be) residual effects of my constant fear of abandonment and quest for love, now, I am able to have a healthy relationship with myself and love myself the way I deserve. I can accept his unconditional love and I can love him unconditionally in return. He is worth it. I am worth it. Real, genuine, from-the-pit-of-my-belly love is worth it.

So each chapter starts off with the story itself, which will start with, "and so the story begins..." The story will then be followed by my thoughts and philosophy about the story, which will start with "and so the contemplation begins..." I'm a little resistant to calling the philosophy part "philosophy." I think it makes me sound arrogant and that's not my intention, but I honestly don't know what else to call it. When I was in high school, I actually considered majoring in Philosophy in college. Until my mother said, "Megan, just because you major in Philosophy does not mean you get to teach your OWN." Well, that's a message from the voices of my past. The Voice of my present day tells me that it IS my philosophy, and I need to simply call it what it is. Philosophy. And to close each chapter, I've included a "moral" of the story.

Please focus on the parts that "speak" to you and ignore the rest. If the story bores you but you really like the "thinking" part, focus on that. If you hate the thoughts but enjoy the story, focus on that. This is as much your journey as it is mine. There are times when it may sound preachy and while that is not my intention, it still may come across that way. Please disregard that which does not move you and please hold onto the rest. Thank you for coming to visit my mind.

Chapter 1

THE MEN IN MY LIFE

Let me start by saying that I'm terrified to do this. I've been avoiding it all morning. Really, I've been avoiding it for 30 years. I have developed some amazing defense mechanisms that have kept me safe all these years, but they are no longer serving me. They are no longer serving me because I am now capable of choosing who I let in my life. I no longer need to simply accept that poor behavior as okay. I can choose. When I was a child, I couldn't. I had no choice. I had to get along with these people. They were the only ones that would keep me somewhat safe. It's the EXACT same mechanism that happened when Van-Boy stole my van (story to be told later). I am the master of re-designing myself to keep myself safe, to get what I want, to get what I think I need. I am a chameleon and the master at skillful manipulation. The problem? Up until now, I didn't realize why I was so good at it and why it has now become so uncomfortable. I am tired of pretending to be happy with the crap I'm being served. I'm ready to order up what I really want from the universe, but until I can break this habit of accepting less than I deserve, I won't be able to read the menu. Or rather, all I will see are the same men in different outfits and with different tastes in music. John Doe, John Doe, or John Doe.

It's all the fucking same...and I've totally lost my appetite.

The current theory is that all of this started with X (a much-older, unidentified male family member who shall be forever known as such) which when put into context, makes a ton of sense. I always idolized him, I wanted to make his life better, I wanted to keep him safe, I wanted him to love me. He was my favorite. He was perfect and he fucked me up. Christ, why on god's green earth would someone send a letter to a kid in high school after not talking to anyone in the family for YEARS? Why would someone put that kind of pressure on a child? He said in the cover letter to the school that it was because he was afraid if a letter from him was received at the house, it would cause my father to have a heart attack. WHAT? That doesn't even make sense!!! Why would he do something that was a total secret from my parents? Over and over and over and over...secrets. All of these secrets. And his secrets were ALWAYS things that made me so uncomfortable. From the beer when I was little, to him leaving me alone in the house to go for a motorcycle ride, to his "truth phase" where he divulged the truth about drugs and diabetes. Oh, and why the fuck did I have to have individual therapy with him when I was in the fucking mental institution after my suicide attempt? (story to be told later) **WASN'T THAT A RED FLAG FOR SOMEONE????????**

And so the story begins...

One of the first memories I have of him and of boys in general was on a beautiful summer evening. X was in his blue bedroom filled with dark brown furniture, a big wood desk, and that "boy" smell - unclean and yucky. His friend was with him. My mother was making dinner and it was time to shuck the corn, a job I hated. So, I went up to see if X would help me. Or maybe it wasn't about the corn. I don't remember. Anyway, I THINK this is when his friend "winked" at me. I had gone in there for something, maybe it was the corn, maybe it wasn't. It doesn't really matter. I turned and ran out as fast as I could. My mother claims that this boy had winked at me and it scared me, and from that moment on, for the next nine years, I was terrified of teenage boys. And we're not talking a normal, healthy fear. We're talking near phobia. I was so afraid that I would cross the street to avoid them. I would cry hysterically when my mother's friend asked me to wake up her son. I did everything I could to stay away from them. I was **petrified** of any boy older than I was, almost until I was a teenager myself. I remember thinking that it was probably not a good thing that I was afraid of them, especially when I would be in high school soon, so I somehow got myself over it. Not that I wanted to, but simply, because I had to. I remember the first time I didn't cross the street when I saw teenage boys I didn't know. I was about twelve. Nothing bad happened. I didn't get hurt. I didn't get attacked. We just passed like ships in the night and I survived. That was the start of me reconditioning myself. I mean, what choice did I really have? I was almost in high school where I would be surrounded by teenage boys. Apparently, all I did was smash all the feelings down. Way down. As deeply as I could and I haven't looked at them since...until now.

And so the contemplation begins...

Now it's become so fucking obvious that I am completely fucked up when it comes to men. I have no idea how to have a relationship with one, and it's stupid X's fault. CHRIST! As I'm writing this, I see myself looking under the rock that is the relationship with X, and then dropping it, and then looking under the rock, and then dropping it. I don't want to do that anymore. I don't want to keep doing the same thing, over and over and over. I want it to stop. I want to smash the shit out of that rock, out of all rocks that hurt little girls. THIS IS SO FUCKED UP. I didn't deserve to have this shit happen. Nobody does. X deserves to be punished and sodomized and hurt and beaten and destroyed. And fuck my father for doing NOTHING. Oh wait, he never did anything. Nobody ever did anything. EVER. I just had to shift my thinking into a way that fit with theirs. FUCK! FUCK! FUCK! FUCK! FUCK! God I hate them. X is evil. My father was ineffectual, and you know what? I don't care why anymore. I don't give a shit about their reasons for sucking so badly. All I care about is: that they did this shit to me, and now I have to pick up the pieces. I'm Humpty Dumpty and they knocked me off the fucking wall. Then they picked me up and did it again and picked me up and did it again. All the while I was on the wall, they told me that I was adorable and cute and wonderful. When they'd knock me off for no reason, I'd be confused and hurt again. So, I'd try to be cute and adorable and wonderful again, ignoring all of their shit, just working to get back into their good graces and it worked. For a little bit. Then they'd knock me off the edge of the earth again. Or throw me over. Or walk away and ignore me completely. FUCK. No matter what I did, it was WRONG.

I was fed this message when I had no choice but to learn it. I'm re-living this story over and over and over and over and over. I don't know why, but I don't feel like I should have to pretend to be anything other than exactly what I am.

~~~~~~~~~~~~~~~~~~~~~~~~~~~~~~~~~~~~~

My father was a steel salesman. Steel. That thing that's so strong and durable and dependable. The thing that my life coach said I wanted wrapped around the velvety insides of my perfect man. Steel. Cold, hard, nearly indestructible. What the FUCK! Who wants that? Why would I want something that unbendable or un-pliable? Strong, sure, but steel? STEEL! I can't imagine snuggling up to a steel beam at night because I'm cold. I can't image my dogs lying beside a lump of steel, hoping for a pet or a kiss. I can't imagine letting something made of steel hold my baby. STEEL! What the fuck! And my father sold this shit. It was his job to convince people, to sway people, to lie to people to get them to do what he wanted...to believe that they could not live without his steel. I learned that skill from every fucking member of my family. And the piece that held my family together, the master of manipulation, the TRUE master, was, of course, my mother. And what did she do for work? She worked in the administrative department at a screw, nut, and bolt factory! THE SHIT THAT HOLDS STEEL TOGETHER! OH MY SWEET JESUS! I was fully surrounded by it! The only problem was that I don't really remember having the cloth option. Let me explain...

There was a psychology study done years ago with a baby monkey. He was taken away from his real mommy and given two surrogate mommies. One was covered in soft, snuggly terrycloth but had no milk. The other one was made of cold, exposed wire but DID have milk. The researchers predicted that the monkey would spend his time with the milk-mother. But they were wrong. The only time he went to her was to feed. The rest of the time he clung to his warm, soft, snuggly mommy. And while this may not seem like much of an experiment, to me (and the researchers) it clearly demonstrates our natural need for touch and connection. We all know we need to eat. That's a given. But do we really consider just how much we need to be touched and loved? This baby monkey got it. And when given a choice, he chose love over food. Interesting.

Oh, and another point worth noting is that my father got sacked from his steel-selling job because he mouthed off to his boss. A man that could not defend his youngest daughter from X or his wife or his daughters got fired because he didn't know how to keep his mouth shut. Again, I must say, WHAT THE FUCK!

~~~~~~~~~~~~~~~~~~~~~~~~~~~~~~~~~~~~

(I paused the writing for a moment outside in the sun. Thought of cigarettes and then watched the shadow of the chain link fence appear and disappear as the sun ducked behind clouds. It was like watching a splash of water dry up and then reappear. Very surreal.)

~~~~~~~~~~~~~~~~~~~~~~~~~~~~~~~~~~~~

Deleted. Gone. As the shadow vanishes and reappears, so does the pattern, the men. Just as I think they are gone for good, I let them slip back in. I let the sun hide behind the clouds. I don't see their hard lines and their false pretenses

27

because the sun, my natural self, is hiding behind the clouds of past messages. When I push the message away, when I shut the Gremlin out, the truth is revealed. It comes blazing down from the heavens of my soul to spotlight the edges that I do not want in my life, allowing me to move on. The idea here is to keep that light on, all the time, so that nobody can ever slip in again. Ever. Why do I not want anyone to slip in? Because they are evil, thoughtless, selfish, careless people.

And to all of you abusers out there: Am I angry? What makes me angry? What puts the cold steel in my voice? Abuse and neglect of people who cannot defend themselves. I will not tolerate it in my presence. I cannot. Be it an animal, a child, a friend, a co-worker. DO NOT OFFER YOUR ABUSE IN MY PRESENCE. I will not allow it. Do not touch those little girls. And the fact that you are even being accused is an indication of something. I do not believe there are very many men, accused, that are truly innocent. Assholes, you have issues! You treat "your" women and children like complete shit. You should be put far, far away from them. I don't care if you didn't do it. It screams volumes about YOU AS AN ASSHOLE that she even believes you might, you could. FUCK YOU! FUCK YOU! FUCK YOU! FUCK YOU! FUCK YOU! FUCK YOU! ALL OF YOU! DON'T TOUCH US! LEAVE US ALONE! I will submit no longer. I do not have to.

And to you father: fuck you for doing nothing about it, you stupid, selfish, lazy, self-centered man. Were you that afraid of my mother to stand up to her? Was she that good in bed? Oh wait, how the fuck would you know? I don't think you ever had sex! WHAT THE FUCK IS THAT ALL ABOUT? There wasn't birth control back then like there is today. She told me she used rhythm all that time, the whole 13 ½ years between me and the next youngest! BULLSHIT! You sat there and took her abuse and dished it right back out to her. All you two ever did was work for each other's love and then push it away. I would do everything I could to get one of the two kinds of love from my parents that I knew. The first (and most consistent) kind was fake and phony and hostile and irritated. It wasn't really love at all. It was really just attention, and negative at that, but some attention was better than no attention. Right? RIGHT??? And when the love was genuine, I didn't trust it. It always seemed like a trick. While I tried to relish it, I was always apprehensive about it. I always knew it could (and would) be taken away at any second, so it made me afraid to be loved. When it came to love, I learned it was easier to have none of it rather than just a small taste of it. It's like heroin to an addict.

   And to you, X, you sick, sick fuck. How could you look into my adoring face, a face that treasured you above all, and HURT ME! And if it

29

wasn't you, then how the fuck could you let your shady friend do it? How could you kiss me with an open mouth when I was twelve? How could you make me ultimately responsible for YOUR relationship with my family? How the fuck could you do that to me? Fuck, you are one twisted idiot and I hate you. I hate all of you. You all did me wrong, you all taught me messed up shit and treated me like I had value when it was convenient, but when it wasn't, I was like a puppy following you around, trying to get you to notice me. I was a nuisance.

If I could have anything I want, right at this moment, it would be to meet New-guy. I would look super cute, and be the sweetest, funniest, kindest, most amazing person he had EVER met. I would flirt and be suggestive, but not too much. I would play right into his hands and then when it progressed, I would shift...

If he asked me if he could see me again, I would say yes but not show up. If he tried to kiss me, I'd let him. Then I'd bite his tongue to the point of blood. A LOT of blood. Or maybe I'd let him kiss me. And then I'd ask him over to my house and let him inside. I would smile at him and slowly walk up to him and wrap my arms around him, kissing him softly. I would take my hand and slide it down his stomach to his fly and rest it there for a second, then start to gently massage him. The kissing would become heavier and more intense and I'd start walking backwards toward my bedroom. The bed would be covered with a special sheet, which would be covering a tarp, a black tarp so that he couldn't see it in the dark of my room. I would start to undress him and slowly take him in my mouth. I would pleasure him until I was certain he was so totally into it that he would suspect nothing. Then I would BITE HIM and not let go. I would allow my jaw to lock and my teeth to penetrate his flesh, sinking deeper and deeper. I can taste the metallic salt on my tongue as it drips down over my lips and onto my bed, leaving a sticky puddle between his legs. His hands would be tied (of course) so he wouldn't be able to truly retaliate (he'd be into it, TRUST me). He would have a gag in his mouth so nobody would hear him scream. I would then take an extremely sharp knife and position it at the top of his inner right thigh, and I would slowly slice from groin down to knee. Slicing the femoral artery like warm butter. Then I would do the same on his left leg, groin down to knee. Then I don't know what I would do…. all I keep thinking about is what it would feel like to reach into his chest with my bare hands and pull his heart and lungs out. I want to squeeze them like jello. I want to feel his insides in my hands, and I want to know that his life is now mine, all mine. I want to absorb his life force as a form of retribution. He is now all men, every single one of them. He is the man, he is all men, he is a man, and he should be dead. He should be destroyed. The gift of life is too good for him and should be given to someone that needs it, that deserves it, that was never given anything more than the chance to draw a breath. It is with his life that I wish to replace the love I am missing. It is the

31

life of others I want to fill this void. It is LIFE. I
WANT LIFE. I WANT TO FEEL ALIVE. ALWAYS.
How can I make that happen without taking it from
another?

       I hate them. I hate them. I hate them. I
hate them. I hate them. I hate them. I HATE
THEM ALL! The men that abuse and hurt and
rape and molest and murder and insult and
penetrate and use and lie and cheat and steal and
live. I HATE THEM ALL! All the stupid idiots
that I have closed my eyes to. WHAT THE FUCK!
THEY ARE THE SAME FUCKING PERSON!
THE SAME WOLF IN SHEEP'S CLOTHING! I
hate them all so fucking much it makes me feel
sick. I can't stop shaking my head in disgust.
They are the same person, over and over and over,
and I hate them all. They are just apes. They are
just alpha males proving their status. They are
gorillas beating on their chests and while these
monkey suits worn by the men in my life change
from man to man, they are still just fucking
gorillas. FUCKING APES! The thought of letting
one into my house makes me feel sick. The
thought of bringing one to my bed makes me feel
ill. I know what true submission feels like. I
know what it's like to be raped and not defend out
of fear. Mr. Lawyer showed it to me. He pinned
me in the back of a cab, with all of his body
weight, and started to kiss me. All I could think
was that if I submitted, he wouldn't hurt me...and

it was awful.

There is another way to submit...by allowing the same type of person back in over and over and over. Karmic debt, with the same Gremlin in a different suit. Well, Gremlin, this debt has been paid. I get it. You got it and you're not gonna get it anymore. This is over. This is done...and it's not going to happen again. Go back to your terrycloth haven. Feeding time is over forever!

What's with the whole dating thing, I wonder. I mean, really. Is it that I just "happened" to pick the same man over and over, or are they REALLY all the same? Does it matter? No, it doesn't. What does matter is that I'm not letting some idiot into my life ever again. They are gonna have to earn me. It's not about making some man make up for the bullshit of all other men. It's about the fact that I fucking deserve something more than I've ever gotten and I am not going to settle for less. I would truly rather bury myself in my work or in my dogs or in my house or in ANYTHING else. I do not want to waste another minute of my time not living. When I allow thoughts of these men, THIS MAN, to own me, I am not living. I am barely breathing because I am so busy waiting for HIS approval, HIS response, HIS possible love. CHRIST, it isn't even the real thing. It's just a hope, a whim, a dream, a maybe. I'm not a gambler, so why the fuck do I go into debt for these slow, non-thoroughbred horses? They aren't even stallions. They are just pathetic, weak attempts at man-dom that cannot handle a truly strong, powerful woman.

Partnership is about being a partner, it's about union, it's about compromise, and it's about trade. And it's all done out of love and a desire to make the other person happy. There is no guilt or manipulation or any of that false, fake, family bullshit. It's pure and real and genuine. When I get nervous about something and my instincts tell me something, I should listen. I am telling myself something, perhaps, something HUGE! Like, STAY THE FUCK AWAY FROM HIM! E-abandonment, while a fabulous and catchy phrase (and very appropriate) does not need to be all encompassing. It can be much more quiet and subtle, like an itch. It does not need to be a full-body breakout. When I don't hear from one of my friends, it pinches my heart a little bit. When I don't hear from one of the MEN, it feels as if there are hooked bungee cords pulled from all angles of my heart, stretched to capacity and then being let go to snap back at me.

~~~~~~~~~~~~~~~~~~~~~~~~~~~~~~~~~~~~~~~

When spending quiet time with the Voice, I am always reminded that the center of the universe is love, has been love, and always will be love. It was like the first time I figured it out while on the tattoo table. The single pinpoint of my mind's eye. It is what offers us light and what gives us clarity of vision. Nothing else matters.

While we collectively need more than just love, it is still the basis and the foundation for all life. It is the story of the baby monkey with the cloth and wire mommies. When a man moves through his life in the pure alpha position, seeking to dominate and own, there are processes going on under the surface that one can only speculate about. My guess is that he's afraid of being alone, afraid of failure, afraid of not being loved. And he's using the skills he learned as a child, as we all do, to get it.

But the amazing thing, today, is that I don't care. I don't give a shit about HIS process or his reason. We are all given crap to deal with, and as children, we don't have a choice. Now, we are children no more. We are adults and I'm sick and fucking tired of adults making excuses for their behavior or expecting something just because they are alive. As children, we should always be given unconditional love and positive regard. As adults, we must earn it by being the best person we can be, by effectively communicating, and by intentionally listening. It is a choice...

New-guy actually emailed me, after two days, to tell me he's been soooooo busy and that he "will" respond to my message. Christ, I have no idea what to do with that, but I can't WAIT to see his response, although it makes me feel nauseated every time an email comes in from him. But that's not new, actually. It's like that every time a virtual man pays attention to me. God, I'm such a fucking open book, so ready to disclose at the first sign of potential trust or interest. I am, totally, setting myself up for failure and pain by doing that and it's got to stop. Just the fact that I'm interested in New-guy's email is bothersome to me. Part of me is just naturally curious, but there's still that part of me that remains hopeful for some fucked up reason. I wish I could say I wish I hadn't "met" him, but I'm actually really glad. He's been a HUGE catalyst for this change in awareness, and I'll be grateful for that always. I still want to say "I think he's a piece of shit", but I really have no idea. All I do know is that THIS is not working for me and it is a huge indicator. FUCK, this sucks. I hate feeling weak.

~~~~~~~~~~~~~~~~~~~~~~~~~~~~~~~~~~~~~

In the dream I had last night, I was right beside the big, wooden table and someone from my dream-family handed me a big, wooden bowl of cucumbers to put on the table. I didn't have to walk over to it or anything, I was just right there, right in front of the table. There were long, heavy wooden benches, not chairs and there were no head chairs. We had to work together to move the benches in and out. But we were all together, all equal. Nobody was more important or less important. It was only together that we could move those benches.

~~~~~~~~~~~~~~~~~~~~~~~~~~~~~~~~~~~~~

MORAL: The pain of a child is easy to ignore if it mirrors our own.

Chapter 2

THE MEN IN MY LIFE – PART 2
(the saga continues)

And so the story begins...

I was 12 and X was 25ish. He had been in the military for four years or so and lived on a base in Germany. When he got out, he moved into my parents' house. I thought he was the best guy ever, which is strange because at the same time I was also afraid of him. It was kind of like meeting a new dog that is really cute and playful and friendly, but you know it has bitten people in the past and could do so again. Anyway, I was super excited to have him back in the house, probably because he paid attention to me, at least until he entered, what is known by my family as, his "truth phase." According to my mother, he had begun to do a good deal of hard drugs and apparently decided that the wisdom he had obtained over the years, his beliefs, his knowledge, was something that everyone would benefit from. Even a little pre-teen girl. So, one day when I was in my bedroom doing homework, he decided to tell me the first in a duet of truths that shook my pre-adolescent reality, which, up until then, had consisted of purple eye shadow, unicorn stickers, and Culture Club albums. I grew up in a very sheltered Midwestern, suburban family. I knew little about anything other than gymnastics, ice-skating, and homework. So, when X decided to tell me that he smoked pot, I was confused and scared. No. Terrified. I was terrified. Drugs were bad, after all. But here was X, one of my heroes, telling me he did something bad, very bad. He told me that he felt it was his job to help me see the world for what it really was, that my parents kept reality from me, and that it was his obligation to show me the truth. I don't remember much about the conversation, except I cried and cried and cried. It was right before Christmas and I was doing a report on a book called "Dog". As we finished talking, he asked me if I wanted to hang out with him on Christmas morning while he got stoned. I was conflicted. Disgusted really, that he asked me to witness that. I wanted to spend time with him, but I couldn't understand why he asked me to hang out while he was doing something that so obviously made me upset. It was very confusing and I didn't know what else to do, but politely decline, because that's what a good little girl does.

The second truth he shared with me while in his "truth phase" was that my father was diabetic. This may not seem like it would be a big secret, but in my family, it was the elephant in the room. X explained that one day when one of my sisters was little, she was snooping through my parents' room. When she got to the garbage can, she found a bunch of needles. Scared and confused, she asked my mother about it, fearing that my father was a drug addict. Did she really even have a concept or was X imagining it? My mother simply said that my father had diabetes and it was never to be discussed it again...and it never was. Nobody ever discussed it. Except for me. Around the same time as X's "truth-phase", my father was experiencing a great number of insulin reactions. (Stress related from X???) I found him in all sorts of places: naked in a pool of orange juice on the kitchen floor, slumped over in the gold living room chair very near coma, thrashing in his bed almost as if having a seizure. Nobody ever, ever discussed it with me. I was expected to just call the ambulance and forget about it. Then, one day, I decided that enough was enough and I was going to **make** him talk to me about it. So I marched into the family room, sat down on the chair beside the Naugahyde couch where he was sitting and said, "I need you to say the word diabetes to me." Stunned (what an understatement!), he said, "**WHAT** did you just say?" So I repeated myself, "I need you to say the word diabetes to me." "HOW...DARE...YOU!" But as the baby of the family does when she really wants something, I persisted and nagged. I stood my ground like no 12-year old should have to. And finally, through clenched teeth, with hands balled into fists so tight I thought he might pound them into my skull, he slowly, painfully, growled "DIE-A-BEE-TEE-ZZZ". I think it was Easter

39

time, because I remember a movie about the crucifixion of Jesus on the TV. Rather apropos. Over the next few years, I continued this forced discussion on this so utterly painful topic for him. Slowly, it became easier and eventually less scary. He seemed to mind it less and less, almost as if I had conditioned him to a point of pseudo-comfort. As a result, I was the only person in the family he could comfortably speak to about it. It was like a secret between just us; I could bring it up in private conversations with him and nobody else was ever part of it. While he hated it at first, there appeared to be some relief in finally having someone to talk to about it, because he would do so freely. It was just us. Huh. Another secret between me and one of the men in my life...

Anyway, after X told me that my father had diabetes, he failed to explain to me what it meant to be diabetic. So, in my 12-year old brain, it meant that my father was going to die. I was crushed and I was terrified. I didn't know how to handle it. It was awful and X did little to pacify my concerns. I don't remember where I learned the right information about my father's condition, but I eventually did.

Another uncomfortable piece of the broken X picture happened around the same time. The room he stayed in was beside mine and he liked to play his music kinda loud. I was a very sound sleeper once asleep, but I had trouble falling asleep if there was any sound. I could obsess about a leaky faucet, snoring, music from another room, etc.. Each time I would ask him to turn it down, he would become angry with me and tell me I was selfish and that it wasn't loud at all. Well, this particular night I just could NOT stop hearing it, so I mustered up all my courage, knocked on his door, and with tears in my eyes asked him to turn it down. He was upset by my upsetness, so he decided to do some meditative guided imagery with me. He tried to use pretty, descriptive words to take me to a mental place of safety and peaceful quiet. It was WAY past my bedtime when my mother realized that he was in my room and I was not asleep. She became very angry and tried to make him stop. I remember hearing them argue in the hallway outside my bedroom, but he didn't give. He came right back in and continued and after they thought I was asleep, which I wasn't, I heard them fighting about it some more.

The final piece of X-induced awkwardness was the open-mouth kiss previously mentioned. I went to say goodnight to him and he kissed me with his lips slightly spread. It immediately sent up "Bad touch! Bad touch!" alerts in my little girl brain, but X would "never hurt me". Right? RIGHT??? Plus, as I've said, I idolized him, so I overlooked his poor behavior yet again.

And so the contemplation begins...

As a result of my years of training to treasure X, regardless of the wrongs he'd committed, I've become an extremely skilled artist and can adeptly construct a picture of who I want a man to be rather than who he really is. I learned how to ignore or overlook anything and everything that contradicted his "greatness". It doesn't matter what the man does or who he is. The image in my head is so real that I see the waking dream instead of the reality. This waking dream is narrated by my Gremlin (a collection of the voices that have programmed us since birth) and he LOVES, LOVES, LOVES it when he's right or can convince me he's right. I hear it over and over, yet, I repeatedly pick unworthy men over and over, simply encouraging my Gremlin. FUCK! I'm so very good at this. How can I ever be trusted with a man...ever? I am so willing to believe anything. Everything. So hopeful. So naive. Am I? Or is it really just that little bastard talking again? You know, I've thought that the Gremlin was exclusively my mother, but it's really a collection of all of them. All the people that showed me for years that I, the natural self that is who I am, was not worth it. Rather, that I was only worth being in one's life for a single and specific reason or for entertainment or "kitschy" value. I am great at being whoever a person wants me to be. I am able to shove the natural-self Megan into a box and lock it up tight. I am good enough for one thing, one reason, and while that reason changes from person to person, the men in my life have always had single focus – the molestation of body, mind, and soul so that I would be a savior, a mother, a caretaker, a therapist... **WHERE ARE THE MEN THAT LOVE ME FOR ME?!?!?!** Where are the men that can handle the intensity and emotion and beauty and enthusiasm? I don't think they exist anywhere but inside my head, with all the perfectly encrusted dreams I create. FUCK. I hate this. I hate this. I hate this. I do not trust men. At all. I believe they all have ulterior motives that involve something that I won't like or that will make me un-whole. I am afraid of them and the power they have over me...or the power I give to them. I change. I shift. I become a mirror of what they want. I become the epitome of their needs while ignoring my own. Will I do this forever? Am I doing it now? Fuck, I can't tell. I never know. I don't know if I'll ever know. Is he the one? Him? How about that one? It's almost comical, the way I move through men, trying them on like suits, then discarding them or allowing myself to be discarded by simply being my natural self. Fuck. They can't handle it; they can't handle me. Can anyone? I know that I operate at full-street pressure. Ever see a broken fire hydrant continuously explode into the air? Yeah, well, my energy is often perceived just like that. Will full-street-pressure freak the next guy out like it does nearly everyone else?

I believe I have an agenda…to find love. To feel love, to be loved, to love. In order to make that happen, I've learned that I must falsify data. I must mentally transform the object (or person, as the case may be) into exactly what I desire, whether it is the truth or not. I do not trust my judgment. I should not be talking to men, but I am unable to stop. And if some new guy can honestly look at my list of must-haves and if he honestly believes it describes him, well then perhaps I'm not as fucked up as I think. No, that's not true. Perhaps he's the prince to break the spell. GOD DAMN IT. There's the fairy tale. SHUT UP GREMLIN!

Okay, hold on a sec. If there is a Gremlin, perhaps there's something that is the opposite of a Gremlin. Wait, I know! It is the natural self! That's the opposite! Maybe that's where the fairy tales live. The Gremlin tries to get me to believe in the ugly, the false, and the painful. The natural self would never, ever, do that. EVER. The natural self wants me to be blissful and enriched and joyful and full and complete. Always. She does not want me to be damaged or full of pain. She views the world through a lens of love. The Gremlin views the world through a lens of despair. I choose the natural self. And if I'm moving through my life in a state of love, love for all beings, then I cannot be hurt, because I am included in all beings. If I am honest and if I love myself and do things because I love myself, I simply cannot be wrong. Trust. I must trust.

MORAL: Abuse, whether it's mental, physical, sexual, or spiritual, is never deserved. However, we learn, in spite of and not because of abuse. It teaches us ways to cope and it shows us strength that we may not have found any other way. There is value in everything. Unfortunately, sometimes we must dig it out.

Chapter 3

AND THEN THERE'S WENDY

When I was first born, I was the center of the universe. I was new and cute and little and everyone adored me. Then my siblings either went away to college or started getting into all sorts of trouble. After that, I wasn't the center of anything or anyone. I was just a duty that must be attended to, like a plant. I meandered through my family, always in search of love and affection. I was no longer a treasure but a nuisance. This is the story of what happens to a nuisance in my family...

The glow from the dining room would gently cascade up the stairs and wash the hallway in a low, gold light. I loved it when that light was on. It meant crescent rolls and my grandmother's china from the dining-room hutch and candles and flowers floating on the rich wood of the dining room table. It meant yummy, juicy ham and green bean casserole with the little onion rings on top and decadent chocolate cake. Most importantly, it meant people. Lots of people. People that would talk to me and smile at me and hug me and treat me like I was a joy to have around. I would look up into the eyes of these grown-ups and feel their love, their glow, their life spill off of them and into me. They would look at me, into me, and love me, just because. I wouldn't have to try to make them care and I didn't have to do anything special. It was just because I was me, because I was just a little girl that deserved nothing BUT love. I felt warm and full and happy. Whole and complete. I was just a little kid, wading through a sea of grown-ups, looking for someone, anyone, to be a buoy of light and love I could hold onto. When that dining room light was on, I knew I was safe. I was surrounded by people that loved me, or at least liked me enough to pay some attention to me.

But when that light wasn't on, when the hallway was dark and the dining room carpet void of a single footprint (my mother was a carpet Nazi – NO FOOTPRINTS ON FRESHLY VACUUMED CARPET), it meant burnt dinner rolls and plain, boring white plates with ugly, little army-green flowers wrapped around the rim, the kind of plates I've seen in at least a dozen other kitchens. It meant dry, tasteless chicken and yucky, slimy lima beans and vanilla ice cream, IF I was being a good girl. Problem was I never really knew what it meant to be a good girl. There were no real rules or guidelines ever explained to me. For me, being good meant that I wasn't made to feel like I was disappointing anyone. The only time I knew I was being good was when nobody was letting anger or frustration roll off them and into me. Part of the confusion was that unless I was in trouble, nothing really rolled off of my parents – no life, no love, no electricity. They were like furniture I was trying to get to notice me and maybe, one day, love me. Every night at dinner, I would sit between my parents. The two people that were supposed to love me more than air or water instead treated me as if I was a nuisance and something that simply had to be dealt with. When I looked up into their eyes, I felt tolerance and distance. I felt cold, empty, and sad. I felt lacking and incomplete. Yet, the harder I tried, it seemed the farther I would get from making them love me. I was like a puppy, chasing after my new owner, doing everything in my power to be cute and sweet and dazzling enough to get a few strokes or maybe a bone. It was never enough. I was never enough. I was always the last of the four kids, with a HUGE gap in between. They had already had their family. I was a byproduct of some random sex act years later (13.5 to be exact). I was an accident. I was a mistake and I spent most of my childhood trying to make up for that, but failing every time.

And so the story begins...

It was Parents' Day at my sister's college. I was just a little girl, only about five years old or so. The regular babysitter, Mary, couldn't watch me during the day on Saturday because she had to work. So my mother got another babysitter, Wendy. Wendy had babysat me lots of times, and I thought she was pretty fun, even though Mary was my favorite. Plus, Mary had the most beautiful dog named Tara. She was a German Shepherd, and I named my stuffed German Shepherd after her.

I was super-excited to have a babysitter all weekend. When it was just me and my parents, nobody played with me or talked to me or pretended with me. My dad just sat and watched TV or read and my mom was always doing laundry or cooking or something. They didn't pay a whole lot of attention to me unless I would bug them, which always worked. At least for a little bit. Oh, but when a babysitter was over, things were different. I had someone to play with and someone to color with and someone to dress up Barbies with. I was the only thing that mattered while the babysitter was there. I was the center of the world and it made me feel elated, joyous, like a red shiny balloon waiting to be let go to float up to the clouds. Boundless energy.

When I was super little, my mother got tickets to the Bozo Show but didn't tell me until the morning OF. She said that was because I would have been so disappointed if something had happened, so it was better to just not tell me. She did that with everything, never telling me what was coming up. In third grade she showed up one day at school and handed me a house key on a thick, brown string tied in a loop. She had a job interview and would not be home after school so I would have to let myself in. I had NEVER gone into an empty house and had NEVER used a key. It's no wonder I never developed patience or a healthy way to deal with scary stuff. My mother just made sure I avoided all scenarios that would require those types of healthy responses and emotions. I never had to wait for anything. As soon as it was real, it was in my face.

So, the weekend my parents left me with the babysitter was springtime. Warm and sunny and sparkly bright. The grass was brighter than a fresh green crayon out of a new box and the sky was a brilliant, flawless, cloudless, crystal blue and seemed like I could almost see through to the other side. Like a window into the heavens. I didn't know that this amazing day, which was supposed to be full of playing and fun, would be fractured to pieces.

It all started with Wendy's friend. She had invited her over for some reason, or at least reasons a five-year old didn't understand, and I was so very disappointed. She was supposed to be playing with me, entertaining me, having fun with me, and paying attention to me. When the babysitter was over, it was all about ME. Only me, nothing and nobody else. I couldn't understand why this was happening, why the person that was supposed to worship me for an afternoon was ignoring me.

Wendy and her friend were in the kitchen laughing and talking about big girl stuff. I was not invited. So I played by myself. Until I had to go potty. I used the downstairs bathroom, something I almost never did cuz it was my parents', but to go all the way to the upstairs one, I would have had to walk past the teenagers at my kitchen table, and I was just too afraid. So, I went in and sat on the pink toilet. The tub was pink, the sink was pink, and the wallpaper was silver and pink. There was a really neat silver mobile hanging over the toilet with boats on it. The rug was gray and it covered the entire bathroom, which was pretty tiny. A silver shower curtain closed off the view to the shower, like the curtain of a stage. It was kind of like being inside a Jeannie's bottle. Or a bottle of Pepto-Bismol...

I was all done, but realized that I had a problem. I had pooped, but my mother still hadn't taught me how to clean myself off. I didn't know what to do. So I sat there for a minute and weighed my options. The only logical option seemed to be to ask for help. So, reluctantly, I called for Wendy and told her I needed help because I had just gone to the bathroom. The two girls erupted into explosive laughter. I was humiliated and wanted to sink into the toilet. But I couldn't do that because I was a big girl. Oh, and I wouldn't fit. So, after my face stopped flushing from the humiliation, I did the best I could, flushed the potty, and slipped outside and away from laughing eyes of the teenagers.

Eventually Wendy's friend left and that's when we started to play house. She said she would be the mommy and I would be the baby and that it was bath time. This is how I remember the rest of that day…

I can see a little girl with long brown hair and big brown eyes standing in ankle deep water in the Pepto-pink tub. The silver curtain of the "stage" was drawn to the left side and Wendy was kneeling in front of the tub. Her hand was wrapped in a washcloth, and she was moving her hand between the legs of the little girl. She was scrubbing and rubbing and hurting her with one of the little girl's parents' gray washcloths. The little girl was crying and asking the babysitter to stop because it hurt. But she didn't stop. She kept rubbing and grinding and hurting the little girl…

Now I can see a little girl with long brown hair and big brown eyes standing on her parents' bed. The room was covered in dark wood paneling and green paisley. There was a big closet full of her mommy and daddy's clothes, except for those they brought to the parent weekend at her sister's college. The babysitter was standing before the little girl with a big, gray bath towel. She was rubbing and drying and hurting the little girl, who couldn't stop crying, which just seemed to make her do it harder and faster. But the little girl just couldn't stop. Crying. Crying. Crying. Crying. Crying. Crying. Crying. Crying….

Eventually, Mary came to take over from Wendy and I was so relieved and happy. Here was someone that I trusted and that I believed loved me. She never made me feel anything but safe and warm and...well, like how all little girls should feel.

I told her what happened with Wendy. I don't remember telling her, so I am pretty sure I didn't make a big deal about it, but more told her like it was just another event in a day in the life of a little girl. But I never told my parents. Ever. I don't know why exactly. Possibly because I didn't think they would care. Possibly because I thought I had done something wrong and I'd be in trouble. Possibly because I was afraid that if I told on her to my parents, she might get in trouble. I really have no idea. What's interesting is that I told the person that showed me unconditional love and compassion, in what seemed an attempt to keep myself safe. Mary of course told my parents and here's how I found out.

A few weeks later, as I rode my bike up to my parents' house for dinner, I saw Wendy and her parents slowly moving across the front lawn toward their car. All six eyes fixed on me as if I was prey that they were hungrily stalking. Their icy stares were full of loathing and revulsion and I had no idea why they all hated me so very, very much. None.

About six years later, I was watching TV at the kitchen table while my mother was cooking breakfast. There was a commercial for a TV show about little kids being molested, so I asked my mother if I had ever been. She said, "Oh sure!

Remember your babysitter, Wendy?"

I was dumbfounded. I had no idea that what had happened to me was "molestation". I mean, that's something that happens to kids with creepy uncles, right? It couldn't have possibly happened to me and if (which was a BIG if) it did happen to me, why the FUCK hadn't anyone talked to me about it! Why did they make me spend YEARS thinking I had done something wrong and that Wendy and her parents hated me because I was bad! Oh, wait...I was bad. I was born and it ruined their perfect little family. I was the reason for all of the problems and stress. I was the reason X started using drugs. I was the reason my sisters went far away to school even though I was told that I was the only reason they ever came home. A lot of pressure for a little girl. I was the reason my mother had to go back to work when I was in third grade. I was just a little girl, for Christ's sake! I didn't know the rules. I've never known the rules with that family! It was like they were some secret club that I couldn't be a part of. I tried and tried to figure it out, to figure them out, but every time I went to the clubhouse door, it was slammed in my face and a "no Megan" sign was hung up. Now, wouldn't it make sense that as the baby in the family, I would have been granted automatic access to the secret club? Shouldn't I have been given love just because I existed? Isn't a mother supposed to play with her child and not just set her in a pile of dirty clothes while she does laundry? Or plop her in front of the TV while she makes dinner? Or send her upstairs to play Barbies so she can read or iron or watch TV or do something, anything other than spend time with her baby? How can a mother be so cold and heartless? How can she look into the eyes of her child that wants nothing but love and affection and still hate her? How can she look into the eyes of her grown daughter and place unrealistic expectations on her and then withhold her love if these expectations are not met? "You should really cut your bangs – only beautiful people like Elizabeth Taylor can get away without having bangs," she would say. How can a grown daughter live with that? Well, here's the thing. I can't. I don't want to. I don't need to. I do not need to be involved with people that have requirements of me in order to give me the love and affection that I simply deserve for existing. When I was sixteen and tried to kill myself for the first time, it was never that I wanted to die. It was always that I wished I had never been born because everything in my family, every bad thing that had ever happened since February 24, 1973, was somehow my fault and the only way I figured out to fix my existence was to kill myself.

And so the contemplation begins…

In my family, good things are never my fault, but rather something that I work to make happen; an expectation of success that I place on myself. It's never my "fault". It's never because of ME. It's because I work hard, or do a good job, or something else that is not directly linked to my existence. I was raised to understand that getting the love from people that are supposed to love me the most, must be worked for. Love is something that is given as a reward and being alive is nowhere near enough to earn that. Being family is not enough. Being kind and sweet is not enough. Nothing I ever did or said was enough. I could have always been more thoughtful or more helpful or less helpful or more patient or more talented or quieter or something, anything other than what I already was. Because I was the fault. I was the failed expectation. I was the reason for bad things. More than a scapegoat, I was the bad thing. I was a task, a chore, a pain, and a problem. I was the bad habit that you can't get rid of. You know you don't want it anymore, but it's still there. Rather than dealing with the consequences of getting over it, you just tolerate it, hating it the entire time. I was my mother's drug. She needed me around so she would have someone that would show her the unconditional love of a child but at the same time that she could emotionally beat like a rag doll. I was an object, something to be dusted and scrubbed and maintained. I was a pet to be fed and washed and walked. I was a thing, something to be looked at but never touched or challenged or stretched. You never want to break your stuff or test its limits or see just what it's made of. It's much better to leave it alone. Things don't change or grow or expand or explore. They are just there. The problem was: that I wasn't a thing or a pet or an object. I was just a little girl whose heart was breaking a little bit more every day.

This isn't just about my mother. My father was present too. Or rather, a man that lived in the house with us. He never snuggled me and rarely hugged me. There was, of course, the obligatory good night kiss, something that I grew to despise, but was my single consistent source of contact with him. Even when I was little, I was forced to settle for "almost" contact. He would nap on the couch and I would take a few of my toys and climb in between his curled-up knees and the back of the couch, like it was my fort. That was my "close" time with him. Even when I was a suicidal teenager, he was useless. I would sit in the living room, reading pages and pages of poetry written in red ink (blood's red, right?) to him, and he would just look at me with these sad, helpless eyes. His youngest daughter was quickly slipping into the black abyss of self-induced death. Yet, he did nothing. My mother did nothing. Nobody that was supposed to protect me did anything. My mother's only way of protecting me was to not tell me something exciting until it was about to happen so I wouldn't be disappointed if it didn't occur. That was my protection.

Why wasn't I worthy of love? What did I do that was so awful? Why wouldn't my siblings ever protect me from them? Why did my mother raise me to hate my father? And to think like her? And to hate mustard? And to believe that her best friend's daughter (who happened to be my best friend and who was my polar opposite – blonde hair, blue eyes, good at things I sucked at) was the better child? Why didn't she play with me? Why did she tell me a few days after my father died that he had always resented me and that I had been a horrible daughter? Why did my sister sit there and say nothing in my defense? Why did she send me the sign from the street I grew up on? Why did she make me feel bad about being depressed and suicidal, like it was a choice I had made and had control over? Why was I molested and never talked to about it? Why did she tell me that the reason I was terrified of teenage boys was because X's friend "winked" at me? That doesn't even make sense! Why couldn't she love me just because I was her daughter? I mean the kind of love that is so powerful, so intense, so amazing, that it makes you cry just because. Its grip around your heart is so tight that it hurts, but just a little. But losing that grip hurts even more, because you become lost and begin to float away into a sea of nothing. The kind of love that leaves a permanent imprint on your heart and in your head, that no matter what, you are never ever without that person. They are a part of you and make you a better person just because you are in their lives and in their hearts. Why do I sit here, alone? Why do I feel so much love, so much love, but have spent my lifetime not understanding how to get it from others? All this time, all I've ever wanted to do is love someone more than anything else. Because that's all I want for someone to do for me. I want to be someone's reason to smile. I should have been HER reason to smile, to be happy, to be joyous, but I wasn't and never will be. I'm just a lost soul to her, as I sit here, sobbing on my laptop, a million miles away, as the falling rain mirrors the tears that spill down my face. I live in California, but I still don't know where my heart is. I need to find it. Somehow.

~~~~~~~~~~~~~~~~~~~~~~~~~~~~~~~~~~

I want to be your rose, forever in bloom. With soft, fragrant petals, promising eternal life and love. I want to be your smile, the crescent moon that shines brightly off your handsome face. I want to be your eyes, the deep hollows of your soul, where I seek out the darkest, most unexplored corners and bring you the answers that you didn't even know you needed. I want to be your hands, every crevice, every crease. The hands that hold what you love so tightly, but loose enough to allow freedom. I want to be your feet that carry you to the window to watch for my arrival. I want to be inside you always. I want to feel your love and be your love and love your love. Where are you and why can't I find you?

~~~~~~~~~~~~~~~~~~~~~~~~~~~~~~~~~~

I've come to realize that my protection has become my demise. The walls I've constructed to keep myself safe are exactly what's keeping the toxicity inside. I need to break down my wall of protection, my wall of safety, if I'm ever to release this poison. My friend advised, "Try your damnedest to remember that the past need not have so much power.", but when the messages heard and absorbed over the years are ones that lack love, and compassion, when the message I have heard from my family is: "you're not good enough", it's nearly impossible. That message has been compounded with repetition over the duration of my life. Only now am I hearing it for what it is and what it means and only now do I see and feel the scars it has left. I was the only child my father was close with. After he died, my sisters told me that the only reason he was nice to me was because I was his last chance at being a good father. Apparently, yet again, something beautiful and wonderful had nothing to do with me as a person, but rather someone else's needs.

This is entirely unnatural on all levels. Not receiving love as a child – not natural. Having to go back in and remove the emotional trash left behind by my emotional polluters – not natural. Getting this out of me, puking onto paper, letting the toxic waste flow through my heart and my head as I release it onto this page – not natural. This ALL goes against what's supposed to happen and is the very opposite of natural. We are designed with mechanisms set in place to prevent us from vomiting, from dredging up the sludge in our systems and spewing it forth. I am going against my own natural grain and forcing this out. I am allowing myself to be completely filled with the pain and ugliness that is my family, allowing it to wash over me. Bathe me. Drown me. Hopefully, I am taking the clean, pure love of the people and animals that are now in my life to cleanse me of it. The "sins" of being unloved will be washed away forever. Having to convince people to love me is unnatural. Feeling as though I don't deserve the love I'm shown because I haven't done enough is not natural. I am asking that these people continue to love me, cleanse me, to make me whole. Love is my redemption. Love is my salvation. Love will set me free from the pain and agony of my past. I will never be free of this damage, these toxins, until I fully release it. It must be released from my mind, from my heart, from my body, from my email, from my cell phone, from my mailbox, from my life.

Love is an addiction of two sorts. There is the unhealthy, suck you dry, bleed your bones, constant urgency and frantic desire kind. And there is the peaceful, calm, make you a better person kind. The first, while seemingly exciting and adrenaline producing simply cannot yield sustained, positive results. It's like being a meth or heroin addict. You will do anything to get your fix. The second, while at first glance is dull, ordinary, and nothing special, is actually long and sustaining, constant and consistent. Non-panic-evoking and beautiful and perfect. I want door number two, please.

MORAL: No matter what, all children want is love. No matter what, some of them just don't get it. No matter what, there comes a time when a child becomes an adult and can decide how much love truly is enough. No matter what, the choice becomes their own and no matter what, the patterns that have been the seasons of life can be changed.

Chapter 4

SUICIDE – A NEAR DEATH EXPERIENCE

Dear Mom - YOU had to be the one to find me. I couldn't let my lifeless, hanging body be found by someone else. It had to be YOU. Because of how much you ignored me, I wasn't going to let you do it that time. I forced you to be involved. It's pretty fucked up when the parent of an obviously disturbed teen says, "I will take you there. I will pay. But I will do NOTHING else" when speaking of getting her some psychiatric help.

And so the story begins...

Circa 1984

I was lying on the steps, upside down, with one of my little gymnastics friends. I asked her if she ever thought about killing herself. I was curious whether or not other eleven year olds did, like I did.

1988 autumn - sophomore year of high school

I got a letter from X, at school, after having not heard from him in YEARS. He sent it to the school because he was afraid if he sent it to the house, my father would have had a heart attack. For the next year and a half, I was not allowed to tell anyone that we were talking and I was the ONLY member of my family that he spoke to. It was this dark, dirty secret that nobody could know about. It made me feel awful, knowing that my parents were worried and wondering and that I knew they didn't need to be, but I couldn't tell them. I had all the answers, but I couldn't tell them. It was a horrible thing to do, to put a child in a position of such power. It was as if X knew he had a trump card – he knew I wanted him in my life but he had no problems making it at HIS conditions. He is a selfish, selfish, man. Once I tried to kill myself, all of that changed, just as I knew it would. I knew that he would be forced to engage with my parents. I just KNEW it. I knew that if I died, he would go to the funeral and see them. I knew that if I lived, he would have to talk to them because I would be locked away. I did this for him. I did this for them. Even after all the pain and torture and feelings of unworthiness, I DID THIS FOR THEM ALL! I did what I had to in order to save **THEIR** family, a family I never felt part of. That was my job. OH GOD. What if that was the entire reason I was born into that family? To save them?

1989 summer – almost a junior

I changed my friends from smart, gifted, skilled, "nerdy" kids to a group that believed being depressed and angsty was normal and "cool." And I was so super cool. So many of these kids put on a show for the adults. "Oh, woe is me. My life sucks. Blah blah blah." Yet they refuse to

66

own up to their own bullshit and make changes. They expected the adults around them to coddle them and become nearly subservient to them. When did the adults lose their balls and let the idiot teenagers run the fucking show? What an utter joke.

Along with changing friends, I also decided I needed a boyfriend to help perpetuate my suicidal plan. That summer I finally got up the courage to call the Italian, the boy I had been lusting over for months. When he got on the phone, I said, "Hello, this is Megan – the girl that everyone says wants to jump your bones." It was love (or some deluded twisted variation of it) at first voice. He immediately became part of the framework of my destruction. Being sad and suicidal was a tolerated and nearly encouraged behavior in my circle. How sick and sad and deadly. How fucking pathetic.

1989 autumn – first semester junior year

The Italian called me at work, told me he was going to kill himself, and hung up the phone. He would not return my calls after that. My friend Onion picked me up, and I became hysterical in her car. Not just your normal teenage hysteria, mind you. This was sobbing from the pit of my belly, crying so hard that pieces of my soul were being shed with each tear, as if it was a layer of skin I no longer needed. Onion drove to Taco Bell because she didn't know what else to do with me. I stumbled through the parking lot, sobbing uncontrollably, finally collapsing into a wet heap in the drive-through. I could not get up. I would not get up. I was hoping the next car wouldn't notice me and just run me over. My friends grabbed me, pulled me up, and dragged me back to the car, where I writhed and moaned in the front seat in pure and utter agony, as if someone was slicing off the top layer of flesh and then bathing me with salt water. I was being tortured.

Onion didn't know what else to do, so she took me to her house. Her mom was a school psychologist after all, so Onion figured I'd be safe. Her mother immediately realized I was falling into a hole that I would never be able to get myself out of, and called my mother telling her that I needed to be taken to a psychologist <u>immediately</u>. Pretty rude for a psychotherapist to tell MY mother how to raise me, HER daughter. The nerve of some people.

When I talked to my mother about it the next day, she said through gritted teeth, "Fine. I'll <u>pay</u> for you to go. I'll even <u>take</u> you. But you're gonna have to make this happen on your own." And just like everything else in my life, I did. Introduce Shrink #1, the man whose heart shattered into a thousand pieces because he couldn't possibly imagine what I was hiding beneath my long sleeves and because of that, was watching me die without even knowing it.

Dec 1989- still first semester junior year

I ditched school to be with the no follow-through Italian and we got caught. I didn't know what to say to the office people, so I told them I was suicidal (true) and couldn't handle school that day (also true). See, all the while I knew EXACTLY what I was doing. I was manipulating the system to encourage the behavior; the action that I knew needed to happen. I needed to try to kill myself. My life could not go on without this. It had become my air. It had become my water. It had become my everything. I was calculating and precise in my flawless plan. I got every single fucking thing I wanted because of it. It was brilliant.

They called my mother, she sent my sister to come get me (God forbid she leave work to tend to her suicidal daughter, the source of her family's demise), and I was admitted into my first psych ward later that night. It was nice, like a hotel. A bunch of spoiled rich kids who simply didn't want to handle their own bullshit anymore, so they acted out and got taken out of the mainstream. All this did was make them even more of a freak and, based on what I saw there, the therapy and growth work that was attempted was a fucking joke. Those kids did NOT get better. They simply learned how to work the system.

They kept me for only two weeks, even though I was a HIGH suicide risk, because my father had crappy insurance. The extremely premature release sent my deadly inferno into an unstoppable rage. Two weeks later I had the Italian give me burns with a Bic lighter on both my arms. I was too drunk to do it myself so he did it for me. (awwww, it MUST have been true love, right?) They were supposed to look like smiley faces, but the lighter got too hot and he held it on my arm for too long. The metal literally melted my flesh and slid down my arm. I picked at it so much that I got a horrific staph infection that eventually went into both of my eyes. After I overdosed and was locked up for real, they told me that if I EVER touched my arm again, they would put me in full leather restraints until it healed completely. I didn't touch it again. Not even once.

Two and a half weeks after the burning (I still have the scars), I was nearly dead by my own doing, so very lucky to be alive with a fully functioning brain.

January 17, 1990

I wore a red and blue flannel shirt that day. It was my favorite. We went to Denny's before school to study for finals, smoke cigarettes, and drink coffee. We sat three booths in from the waiting area. Even now all these years later I can see that day, that hour, that greasy diner from my own eyes. I am not even entirely sure who I was with. Probably the Skinhead, the Italian and K, but I don't know for sure. The Skinhead was my best friend at the time. She was one of those girls that I had wanted to be friends with so very badly. So one day, when she was walking through the lunchroom, full of angst and depression, I offered her a piece of gum. That's all it took.

It was time for class, so we left. I have no idea which final exam I had that day, but I didn't care then and I most certainly don't care now. What did matter was that, because of finals, we all got out early and went to the mall. It seemed like my friends were worried about me because I was so very and so clearly out of sorts all day. I was in that distant place that allows people who know me to know I'm not really present. I'm accounted for, but I'm not engaged. I'm gone and inaccessible to anyone. When people try to pry me from my place, I come halfway out, for just a minute, and then slip back in to my numbness. At the second they disengage, for even a breath, I'm gone again. This is a place where I go to think. I imagine. I daydream. I'm safe. It's warm. Nobody's in there with me telling me that what I'm thinking is weird, stupid or just doesn't matter. But I've got to be totally honest; it's not REALLY a safe place. It's more of a round room, with no doors or windows. The only art on the walls is what my imagination draws at any given moment. It is lit with torches and there is a single chair in front of a table. It is where I write. If someone were to come into that space, it would feel as if they were waking me up or maybe pulling me from dark, mucky waters where I appeared to be drowning. And sometimes, I was...

Even though it was getting late and we all had finals the next day, my friends wouldn't take me home. I never said I wanted to go home, but I remember wondering why we were STILL hanging out at the mall. It seemed like they were afraid of what would happen once they weren't with me. These people, these "friends", all seemed to know that I was in trouble and I was sinking, but nobody reached into the water to see if I needed a hand. These people were just like all the other people in my life. They were bigger than me, stronger than me, and made of stone. They were bodies with no heads or heads with no bodies. They were the lumbering monsters of Stonehenge: cold and hard and gray and thoughtless. They were put there with intent, purpose, thought, and design, but after they were there, their purpose was lost. Just as I was lost. I was just a tiny girl wandering around these huge monstrosities. I had put them there to make myself feel safe, but all they did was keep me from safety. They isolated me and secluded me. Mocked me with their pretend love and their pretend concern. They were nothing more than stone legs I had to maneuver through while I was searching and crying out for something real. I needed something warm, something pulsing with life. Yet, I was always alone in that fucking circle.

ALWAYS.

By the time they dropped me off, it was really late and I didn't have time to study for my final on the next day. Once I realized this, the axe fell and my pendulum of suicidal ideations was launched into full-blown, explosive action. All because I didn't want to fail my final. I mean, how on earth could I fail a final exam? Outstanding academics were an unspoken expectation in my house, but very expected nonetheless. Failure wasn't an option. It wasn't even discussed. It was just known that good grades must happen. My oldest sister did it. My next sister did it, but never quite as good as the first. My brother did it, so, rather than give my household the chance to scold me or punish me or even worse, to be disappointed in me even more then they always were, I decided to quit and not give them the chance to hurt me anymore. I figured that if I quit, they couldn't fire me. HAHA! I win! Wait...I win?

I called Onion and told her I loved her, and while the sentiment and statement were not particularly unusual, the call was late, random and out of the blue. I was born with the ability to communicate psychically, heart to heart, soul to soul, but my family of origin was nothing but inanimate objects. Legs of stone and wood and pain. Since that was all I was conditioned to know, the people that I picked to be in my life were also inanimate objects of stone and wood

73

and pain. When I would try to communicate to any of them, the energy I exuded simply bounced off of them and back and into my heart like a lightning bolt. So, I learned to communicate verbally, through written and spoken word, as if it is a second language. It's almost as if I'm constantly translating the beauty of the truth I know and feel and hear in my heart into some inadequate, incomplete sign language that can only convey a fraction of the true emotions that lie beneath.

I put on my coat, went outside and smoked some pot, and then walked down to a park across the street from my grammar school. The place where I fell off the monkey bars and got a mouthful of sand. The place where I got in trouble for calling a girl a "bitch" because she was being mean and hurtful to my friend. The place where EVERYONE laughed at me after I got a perm. The place where I threw up on my teacher's shoe. (I didn't mean to. I was simply waiting in line to tell her I was sick, and to ask what I should do. In my house, I wasn't allowed to do anything, even barf, without asking. Only, that time my question didn't come soon enough.) The place where I learned that my mother was going back to work for the first time. I hated that stupid, fucking school. I'm sure it wasn't a coincidence that I did it at a park across from the school. This way the teachers wouldn't find me, but the other kids would, and they couldn't yell at me or get me in trouble. I was somehow "safer" with them instead of the big, stone legs of the grownups, the legs I navigated through during all of my growing-up years. The kids were just little stone legs and were much easier to get around...or knock over.

My plan was to hang myself. So I took my coat off, took my shirt off, put my coat on, made a makeshift noose out of my shirt, attached it to the jungle gym, and slipped my head into it. As I hung there, I began to feel the life slowly lift out of my body and hover just above me. I was terrified of succeeding and yet, I was terrified of failing. I couldn't do it. I knew I wasn't supposed to die there, like that. I tried, I really did, but as the life started to slip out of me, I got scared and let myself fall to the ground. It really wasn't a very good noose anyway. Besides, I wasn't allowed to do anything without my mother nearby and I couldn't punish her well enough from afar. So I walked home.

I got into the house and told my mother I needed to run to the store so she gave me the keys to her car. I went to Walgreen's and bought three boxes of different types of sleeping pills. I was afraid they wouldn't let me buy all three and I didn't have any sort of alibi, but they didn't care. They were just more faceless, nameless stone people, mini microcosms of the huge, lumbering monsters that surrounded me.

~~~~~~~~~~~~~~~~~~~~~~~~~~~~~~~~

I had been trying to get caught for YEARS yet nobody seemed able to catch on. I had been writing exclusively with red ink in my journals. I had been writing poetry about death and destruction, MY destruction. I had been sharing this with anyone that would listen. I wore all black. I hung around with kids that wore all black. We wore combat boots and stomped around school and the clubs and the mall, making sure everyone that saw us knew just how pathetic and miserable our lives were. I was SCREAMING, CRYING, WRITHING for years. Nobody cared. Nobody.

~~~~~~~~~~~~~~~~~~~~~~~~~~~~~~~~~~

I got home with my bundle of pills, said good night to my mother, (for what I assumed would be the last time), and marched up to my room with the boxes and a huge cup of Sprite (a soda my mother and I both didn't really like – but she always bought stuff that she didn't like so that it was easier to not eat it). I grabbed a flashlight, turned off my light so my mother wouldn't know I was still awake, and sat on my bed cross-legged. One by one by one, I pushed each little pill out of its cellophane package and made three piles. There were probably ninety pills total laid across my bed. I then wrote my note. The symbols I assumed to be the last words I would ever write were placed in my desk as I looked up to "God" and said, "This is now up to you." I calmly began to take the tiny blue and white pills one by one by one.

By the time I got to about sixty pills, I had to go to the bathroom. I had a weird fear of being found in a wet bed for some reason, so I struggled to stand and stumbled toward the door. I fell to the floor and when I tried to reach for the doorknob, I was just a few inches shy. It felt like someone was holding my arms down and I had to use all my might to lift them at all. Then Suddenly, the doorknob started to turn, from what I assumed was my sheer will. My mother pushed open the door, took one look at me in a pile on the floor, and cried out, "Oh my god. MEGAN! What have you done?!?!" For some reason, I said, "Don't worry Mom. I just took some acid. Everything will be fine in the morning" (NOTE – I had never taken L.S.D. at this time so why I used that excuse, I have no idea). I miraculously stood up. Using my super-human determination and stubbornness to lift my body, I gave her a hug, and she went back into her room.

Now, why she just left me there and did NOTHING is beyond me. I have no idea what that woman was thinking. EVER. My guess is… "How can my daughter be doing this to ME???" Because it was always about HER. It was never about me. EVER. HER. HER. HER. HER. HER. HER. It was so much about her, that she trained us kids to HATE my father because she resented him and because SHE wanted to be the favorite...she needed to be the favorite.

Anyway, I stumbled to the bathroom, peed, and then I slipped into blackness. I somehow made it back to my bedroom only to land flat on my back on my bed, dying. Sometime later, my mother said she heard me choking and struggling so she came into my room, grabbed my newly dyed black hair, pulled me up, and allowed me to vomit; allowed me to live. God, she'd given me life twice...only, the second time, she blocked out the fact that it even happened! What an ungrateful, spoiled, rotten brat I am!

The next thing I remember is lying on the gurney in the ER, really low to the ground. I looked up and saw a woman shuffling down the hall with a walking IV. She was crying and all I wanted to do was give her a hug. It's possible that this is nothing more than a hallucination, but I swear if I saw that woman today, I'd know her immediately. And I would walk right up to her and hug her like she'd never been hugged before.

I have no memory of the first day in ICU – of the psych tests, the tubes or the nurses. Not even consciously being alive or dead, I was in a space of nothing, of non-existence. It felt like my mind was on vacation while my spirit was deciding what it wanted to do. Luckily, it chose to live.

When I woke up, I couldn't move my arms. I thought that they had become paralyzed as a result of taking the pills. Remember how I couldn't reach the doorknob? GREAT. Not only had I failed to kill myself, but now I'm fucking paralyzed. Yeah, good one! Well, turned out that I was NOT paralyzed, but they had tied me to the bed because I was textbook "crazy". I imagined people in the bed with me, but not the whole person. Just their decapitated heads. If it's just a head, it has no heart, and if it has no heart, how can it REALLY love me? It can't. It won't. It's just like the fucking stone legs. God, I hate those fucking things. The Italian stood from the neck down against the wall in my room. Just a body. If it's just a body, it has no head, and if it has no head, how can it know it really loves me? It can't. It won't. Again, the fucking stone legs. God, I hate those fucking things. People were talking about me in the nurses' station and standing in the corner of my room. Just voices. If it's just a voice, it has no head and no heart, and if it has no head and no heart, how can it REALLY love me? It can't. It won't. It's just like the fucking stone legs. God, I hate those fucking things. I was surrounded by all of the parts of people that couldn't possibly love me. Hearts with no heads. Heads with no hearts. Bodies with neither. If it's just one piece and not the others, how can something so utterly incomplete REALLY know or feel or understand that it loves me? It can't. It won't. It's just like the fucking stone legs. God, I hate those fucking things.

I was in agony. I was struggling. I was wishing for death. They had to keep me tied to the bed to prevent the ideation from turning into action for a second time. When I was finally able to convince them that I was okay and wasn't going to do anything bad, they untied me. I tried to crawl out of bed to go to the people I was seeing. Like always, they weren't REALLY there. I struggled to gain equilibrium, but I knelt on the tube of my catheter, nearly ripping it out of me, and I decided that I'd better just stay put in my bed.

Later, I felt like I was choking on the tube shoved down my throat to pump my stomach, so I pulled it out. With my bare hands. All the way. My nurse Eden came running in and said, "Megan, what have you done?!?!" I looked at her and innocently asked if she wanted me to put it back. Eden said not to, so I tossed the tube across the room. Huh, wonder why they thought they had to keep me tied down. I seemed pretty stable, didn't I?

The next morning, I woke up to see a blur of royal blue beside my bed. As my eyes adjusted, I saw my mother's face tucked up on top. She was not just a body or just a head, but they were not entirely connected, as if they could exist without each other.
She looked like an angel, with a kind, sweet smile shining down on me, like a ray of sunshine. I looked up into her face and said, "Mom, can I touch you?" She said "of course", but wanted to know why. I said, "Because I want to make sure

you are real." I reached out to her, placed my hand on her coat, and knew that I was coming out alive.

I remember my psych tests that day. Fire trucks are red. I'm in the hospital. It's 1990. 1 plus 1 equals 2. They finally let me get out of bed. I gingerly walked over to the sink and looked at myself in the mirror for the first time since days before and possibly, for the first time in my life. I stared into my face and looked directly into my own soul. My skin was white. My hair was black. I looked like a corpse. I began to cry.

And so the contemplation begins...

Suicidal ideations? At eleven? I was ELEVEN when the thoughts began! HOW CAN A CHILD BE SUICIDAL FROM THE TIME SHE'S ELEVEN AND HAVE NOBODY DO A GOD DAMN THING ABOUT IT????? OH WAIT, I KNOW. IT'S THE SAME REASON I HAVE A MOTHER THAT DOCUMENTED IN MY FUCKING BABY BOOK THAT I WAS AFRAID OF TEENAGE BOYS AT THE AGE OF THREE, because THAT'S so normal! Why did I have to ASK my mother if I could touch her? She wasn't holding my hand or sitting beside me or lying with me in my bed? I should NOT have had to ask to touch my mother! By having to ask, I was not only validating her presence in the physical sense, but also in the spiritual and maternal sense.

81

If that had been my daughter in the bed, I would not have left her side, I would have been touching her, I would have been holding her, I would have made damn sure she knew, beyond any shadow of a doubt, that she was LOVED. Instead, my mother had conditioned me to ask for everything and anything I wanted. If I wanted a glass of water. If I needed to be excused from the table. If I wanted to change the channel. If I could eat a cookie. LOVE, most certainly, wasn't just handed out. It must be earned. It was a reward for something done well. Apparently a failed suicide attempt is just that...failure.

I wish that my mother would acknowledge the fact that she saved me that night. It was the one most important thing she ever did right throughout my entire life. To this day, she still refuses to believe that it happened. Just like always, avoidance of things unpleasant was her mode of operation, and even twenty years later, those cold stone legs still find ways to stomp on my heart. Even from 1500 miles away...

ARGHHHHHHHHHHHHHHHHHHHHHH HHH!!!!!!!!!!!!!!!!! I feel like I'm going to be sick. I never had anyone love me the way I deserved. EVER. Oh my god. Oh my god. How can a parent watch her little girl slide deeper and deeper into a place she can't get herself out of and DO NOTHING! FUCKING NOTHING!!! I was worth nothing. I was nothing. I was a nuisance. I wonder if they partly wished it would happen so they wouldn't have to deal with me anymore. It was never that I wanted to die. EVER. It was always that I had wished I had never been born. And the only way I knew to fix that was to die. Everything was my fault, my whole life. It was my fault that X became a drug addict. It was my fault that my baby sitter molested me. It was my fault that my sister moved to Colorado and lived with her boyfriend before marriage. It was my fault that my other sister moved in with her boyfriend before marriage. I was the reason for the collapse of my family. I was the reason. It was always my fault. I was the reason for everything. From my siblings wanting to come home (per my Mother, "you know the only reason they come home is to see you") to the reason my father was a miserable man (per my mother, "you were a bad daughter and he always resented you").

So, why suicide? Why not running away or cutting or something else? I think a large part of it was because I needed to know that I had purpose here. I NEEDED SOMEONE TO CARE WHETHER I LIVED OR DIED!!! I gave my life to the Powers That Be the moment before I swallowed the first pill. I trusted Them to do what was right, and I trusted Them to get me what I needed. If I had run away, it wouldn't have turned out the way it was supposed to. I was supposed to try to take my own life. It was simply my destiny and nothing else fit into the puzzle of my existence...and the Powers That Be proved their love for me. They made me feel like I had worth and a reason to be here...even if I didn't know what that reason was. Until now. I believe in Them just as They believe in me.

MORAL: With a clear objective, it is possible to get positive results with negative behavior. Only you get to decide what is positive for YOU.

Chapter 5

THE VAN

And so the story begins...

Onion said to me, "If you go to Louisville and you get back together with Van-boy, I will never speak to you again." And she never did...

I knew the odds of finding Van-boy at the Dead show in Kentucky, which was part of the reason I wanted to go, even though NOBODY wanted me to ever see him again. He treated me like shit for years but I still "loved" him. I don't know why, but I did. It doesn't matter why, really. What matters is that I knew where I could find him and I trusted that instinct.

When we rolled into Louisville for the Grateful Dead shows, I patrolled the lot. I said that I was looking for one of our friends, but I was really looking for Van-boy. When I didn't find him, I was very disappointed so we went into the show.

Afterwards, as my friend and I were walking back to the car, I spotted Van-boy's jeep. Anyone that had spent any time in it would not forget it. There was something undeniably unique about it. It was tan with a million Dead stickers plastering it together. A total piece of crap and so very much like him. As soon as I saw it, I started to shake and cry. While I had no idea what I would do or say if I saw him, I felt like I just had to let him know that I knew he was there. So, we walked over to the jeep and I left a note on his windshield, asking his car neighbors to tell him I had stopped by. And then as we started to head back to our car, there he was. Van-boy. Everyone and everything else disappeared and he was all that I saw. I was fully engaged and focused on him and there was nothing that would prevent me from reaching him. I didn't run and I'm not even sure if I increased my pace. What I do know is that it felt like I was floating. He was before me at last and my heart was singing.

I honestly don't remember his reaction to me at all. I have no clue. What I do remember is that he took me to sleep with him at his father's boat. We didn't have sex. I'm not even sure we kissed, but we snuggled and it was wonderful just to be beside him again. The next day we hung out together doing a bunch of nothing and I got back to the show late. I had my friend's ticket and felt terrible that I couldn't find her. I was beside myself and felt very selfish for having not been where I said I would be when I said I would be there. Instead I was with Van-boy. Because of this guilt, I decided that it would have been wrong for me to go into the show without my friend, so I held both tickets and waited outside, just so I could show her that I really felt awful. Van-boy was pissed that I wouldn't let him take one or both tickets. Just like him…thinking only of himself.

The run of Louisville shows was over, and it was time to go. I said goodbye and was no worse for the wear. I had survived seeing him. I felt strong, in control, and powerful. Very different from how I was used to feeling around him, but that wouldn't last.

I finished the tour and ended up in Pennsylvania with some curly-haired boy, sort of stuck in his wacko mother's home. My plan was to stay for a few months, earn some money, and then head out to Oregon to live with some of the curly-haired boy's friends. Sometime during my stay in Pennsylvania, Van-Boy had turned my "friendly" conversations into "I love you" dialogues. I had no intention of that happening and I have never really been sure of how he did it. I just remember standing in the psycho mother's kitchen and telling Van-boy that I loved him and that I'd see him soon. So my new plan was to drive down to Louisville, pick Van-boy up, and bring him out to the West Coast with me. He has always wanted to go out West and it made sense to have someone along for the ride. I had no fears of what would happen. It all just seemed so logical. After all, I was a young girl on the road all alone. I needed him there. Right? Right???

The drive from Pennsylvania to Kentucky was actually kind of pretty. I went through Ohio and was amazed at the scenery, but this outer beauty did not dissipate my increasing angst. With every spin of the tire, my heart became heavier and heavier. I had no idea what to expect and wasn't sure where I stood with Van-boy. I was trying to maintain my composure and keep it so that I would just roll with whatever happened. Again, I was just lying to myself.

I arrived in Kentucky an hour before I was expected. But did I call him??? NO! I was too afraid he wouldn't be there; just like he wasn't there soooo many times I had called him over the years. This was not the first time in our relationship that I had changed everything in my life to accommodate his plans and I was terrified that he might just crush me again. So, I sat at a marina and waited for the longest hour of my life to pass. When it was "officially" time for me to arrive, I called him and he gave me directions to his house. When I got there, he opened the door. His watered-down-cola colored hair was wrapped in tiny braids. While I thought the braids looked stupid, his beautiful emerald eyes made his face utterly perfect. And suddenly I didn't really care about his stupid braids at all. It was Van-Boy standing before me, after all, and I would have moved the earth for him.

He gave me a hug but no kiss. We talked, but did not touch. When it was time for bed, he offered me his room and he stayed on the sofa in the living room. Even at the time I thought it was strange, but I gave him the benefit of the doubt, believing, hoping that he was just being thoughtful and waiting to see how things were going. What an idiot I was!

The next morning we decided to take my car and trade it in for a bigger vehicle, making a cross-country road trip easier, as he had a big German Shepherd. So we left his house and headed into town. As I drove us down the highway, he suddenly leaned over and gave me a kiss. I felt (or imagined?) passion and intensity and desire. All of my worries melted away and I started to believe that his one small action confirmed my hope that he was just being patient for my sake. What an idiot I was!

He had an auto dealer in mind and when we got there, we saw this totally awesome 1976 Ford E-150...a total "hippy" van. It was gold and red with murals of Indians and sunsets and teepees all over it. The inside had red and black shag carpet and red velvet captain's chairs. There was an icebox and wood poles splitting the front from the back. It was the coolest van I had ever seen and it was SUPER cheap! Only $750!!! Now, I had a 1991 Toyota Tercel, paid for in cash by my parents who were dumb enough to give me the title before I left home to follow the Dead. I traded in my car for about $2200 (total!!!!) and left with a handful of cash AND a super cool van! I was in HEAVEN!

I had never in my life driven anything quite so big, so he was designated captain. The front end was really messed up and he had to move the wheel like he was driving a boat. When I DID try to drive it, I couldn't keep it in the lane and almost killed us by nearly rolling into a tree-filled ditch. But at least there was an ice-box. Right?

We knew the front-end had issues, hence the "driving a boat" feeling, so we decided to have his uncle take a look at it. His uncle's house was also the home of his favorite cousin, who also happened to be one of his closest allies. As the three of us (Van-boy, the cousin, and I) were hanging out, the cousin's little girlfriend and even younger sister came over. The five of us were just talking about nothing, and the next thing I knew, the four of them left me and went inside. I don't remember it bothering me all that much at the time or maybe I was just doing a good job of ignoring it. However, I do remember it crossing my mind that I felt a little bit like a fifth wheel. What an idiot I was!

After the four of them were gone for a while, Van-Boy returned and asked me if I wanted to go camping. We had no other plans, so I thought it would be fun. As night descended and we prepared to head out, we stopped to get gas. Van-Boy and I were in my van and his cousin and the little girls were in his car. I jumped out with enough money to pay for the gas and buy cigarettes, along with my toothpaste and toothbrush. I ran inside and then to the bathroom. After I cleaned myself up and paid at the register, I moved toward the door only to notice that the gas station was seemingly empty and that there were NO vehicles or people at the pumps. NONE. NOBODY. Not my van. Not Van-Boy's cousin. Not the little girls. It was just me.

Without even thinking, I simply moved through the door and headed left to the back of the parking lot. There was a blue mailbox and I sat beside it, as far away from the door as I could. I didn't want anyone to see me and to know what had just happened. I didn't cry. I didn't scream. I didn't move. I didn't think. I didn't breathe. I just sat there, stunned. I was in total shock and could barely even begin to fathom the fact that Van-Boy and his little friends had left me in the middle of nowhere Kentucky with nothing but the clothes on my back, five dollars in my pocket, two packs of cigarettes, and my toothpaste and toothbrush. All of my money, my clothes, and all of my stuff was in MY VAN and I was stuck at some fucking gas station, all alone, totally abandoned.

I must have sat behind that mailbox for nearly an hour, just watching and waiting for him to come back...he was just taking them for a ride in the van after all. Right? Right??? He'll come back. He wouldn't just leave me here. Maybe he forgot which gas station I'm at. I should probably go sit by the road on those bags of fertilizer. I can see the highway for a long way in both directions. He'll come back. He'll see me and come back for me. Right? RIGHT???

As I climbed onto those fucking bags of

fertilizer, something inside me started to shift. The shock began to slide away and my nerves, raw and exposed, began to show. With every second that slowly clicked by, my "deer in the headlight" feeling was being replaced with the seeds of anger. And resentment. And frustration. And hatred. And disgust. And rage.

The rage pulled me up off my ass and walked me over to the payphone. Yes, back then we did not have cell phones. We actually used quarters to call people if we weren't at home. So, I called the only person I knew in that ENTIRE state! Van-Boy's aunt, the mother of Van-Boy's shithead cousin.

She answered the phone as if I had woken her from a bad dream. "Hello, this is Megan. Van-Boy and your son have stolen my van and everything I own and I need you to come get me. NOW."

"Uh, Megan, it's really late."

"Yes, I KNOW it's really late. I'm standing at a gas station with nothing but the clothes on my back and two packs of cigarettes. You need to come get me NOW."

"Oh, I just don't….."

"Look, if you do NOT come get me NOW, I will have your son arrested as an accomplice to grand theft, auto."

I KNEW I had her. The cousin was an off and on again troublemaker and she would NOT want this on his record. She reluctantly and begrudgingly agreed to pick me up. As soon as I got off the phone with her, the rage forced me to pick the phone back up and call the police. A squad car was sent over nearly immediately and arrived well before Van-Boy's aunt. I told the officer the details of what happened and when I was finished, he asked me how I wanted to file the complaint: unauthorized driver or stolen vehicle. The difference, according to him, was that if Van-boy got caught as an unauthorized driver, he would not be arrested because it was only a misdemeanor. Which do you think I picked? Just like any moron would do, I was working diligently to convince myself that he would come back..."um, unauthorized driver please". WHAT A FUCKING IDIOT!

I climbed into the aunt's car and sat in stunned silence. My brain was moving so fast it wasn't even moving anymore. It felt like my world had been put on pause and fast forward simultaneously. When we arrived at her house, I slipped out of the car, wandered in my dazed fugue into the house and sat on the couch, seeing nothing in front of me whatsoever. Auntie and Uncle lit up a joint and asked if I wanted any. I was shocked that at a time like this, the MOST stressful time in my life, the thought of getting me stoned crossed anyone's mind. I (politely?) declined, kept my thoughts to myself, and lay down on the couch. I was asleep before my head even hit the cushion.

I woke up the next morning, very reluctantly. Sleep was a much happier place to be than my alert, conscious brain. The brain that knew full well what had happened. My sleep brain could trick me out of believing the truth. Sleep was my dream and awake had become my nightmare. The sunlight and the noise from the kitchen forced me to open both of my eyes all the way and greet the horrific truth square in the face. The person that was supposed to love me the most had abandoned me in the worst possible way. Abandoned. I had just been totally abandoned.

I sat, listless on the sofa that had become my boat in this sea of uncertainty, terror, and despair. It was as if it was a rock that I was clinging to for dear life. I could not move until a low, recognizable rumble stirred the air, barely audible. It was down the street but getting closer, closer, closer, closer, closer. It was in front of the house! I grabbed my backpack and started running through the front yard toward the street, toward my van, and toward my life, but the moment he saw me, he DROVE AWAY! ARGH!!!!!!!!!! I had fucked it all up, I had scared him away! Had I just kept my dumb ass inside, he wouldn't have known I was there and would have come IN! DUMB FUCK! I ran back inside, the adrenaline pumping through my veins, my heart raging in my chest, my breath coming in frantic gasps. I grabbed the phone and called 911.

"HE'S GETTING AWAY! HE'S GETTING

AWAY! HE'S GOT MY VAN! PLEASE COME GET HIM! PLEAASSSSEEE!!!!!!!"

The voice on the other end, in a sssllllloooooooowwwww southern drawl, said, "Well ma'am, your van is listed with an "unauthorized driver" and not as stolen, so I can send a patrol car over, but it won't do much good."

"HOW DO I CHANGE IT TO STOLEN?" ARGH!!!!!!!!!!!!!!!!!

The sssllllloooooooowwwww southern drawl said, "Well ma'am, you'll just have to come down to the station with your ID and make the change."

"BUT HE STOLE MY ID!!!!!!!!" ARGH!!!!!!!!!!!!!!!!!!!

The sssllllloooooooowwwww southern drawl said, "Well then you'll have to wait until Monday and go talk to a judge about that there. There ain't nothin' we can do for you."

ARGH!!

I slammed the phone down and started pacing. Then as if on cue, the cousin and his little girlfriend (minus the little sister) came strolling into the house. They were not expecting to see me and their surprise was obvious. Although, where they thought I would go, I have NO fucking idea.

They both started going on and on about how sorry they were, how they didn't know what had happened, BLAH BLAH BLAH BLAH. Then the little girl says to me, in her stupid, hick, ass-backward Kentucky drawl, "I understand just how you feel."

"WHAT did you just say to me? You UNDERSTAND, you stupid little bitch...YOU UNDERSTAND?!?!?!"

Pure and unfiltered rage began pulsing through every inch of my body and I was suddenly consumed with the most intense blood lust I have ever known. I grew to about ten feet tall, and slowly started moving in toward that sweet, stupid fucking girl. Oh, how good it would feel to snap that pretty little neck with my bare hands, watching the panic and terror bleed from her eyes in salty tears, while HIS cousin, HER boyfriend, the father of her unborn child WATCHED! I could feel her flesh in my hands; I could feel her pulse throbbing into my warm, dry palm. I was calm. I was ready. I was murderous. I started slowly moving in toward my prey, ready to taste sweet death on her lips, when THEY saw the look in my eyes. They were from the country. They were hunters. They knew blood lust. I was like an animal that had found the most perfect, the weakest, and the most delicious victim I could have ever hoped for. And she was so fucking stupid that she actually started moving **toward** me, ready to dance with me! My prey was walking TO me!!!! OH MY GOD! What a fucking idiot!

They knew that I was going to do serious and totally irreversible damage and so they started moving toward me, too. Then suddenly time stopped for a moment, and I had a flash of brilliance: these stupid, ass-backward idiots were the ONLY people, my ONLY potential allies in the whole world. What would happen if I killed one of them? Who would help me then? I'd be utterly alone and HE would win. I could not have that. WOULD NOT have that. So I stopped, suddenly, and flipped everything around. Instantly.

"Oh my gosh, I'm so sorry. I'm just so upset right now. I didn't mean to call you names. BLAH. BLAH. BLAH. " And the stupid ass-backward hillbillies bought it! BAHAHAHAHAHAHAHAHAHAHA!

The cousin and his little girlfriend felt like total shit (or so they said), like complete assholes (or so they pretended). They knew I knew that they knew I was abandoned at that gas station and they were serving penance. It was priceless. I was hungry, so they took me to Taco Bell. I needed to go to court on Monday, so they were gonna take me. They would do ANYTHING I wanted. I owned them. They all became my prey without me having to shed a single drop of blood.

As I was playing cat and mouse with the most idiotic and stupid mice EVER, I began to inquire about Van-Boy. Where was he? Where'd he go? What was he gonna do? Was he okay? His cousin, being the idiot that he was, told me everything. Van-Boy was on his way up to Chicago. He had court and was going to use my money to pay restitution on the grand larceny charge from a few years earlier. (Nice clue I overlooked, don't ya think?) His cousin figured he was gonna come back to Kentucky after that was all situated. He also told me that Van-Boy was supposed to call that afternoon. So I asked if I could go with so I could talk to him. What could he say really? "No? You can't come? I was party to grand theft auto of your van and to your total abandonment, but you can't come with?" Please. No fucking way. He was my puppet and I knew I'd be talking to Van-boy later that day.

So, we all drove over to Van-boy's mother's house, and after a few hours, Van-boy called and I ripped the phone out of his cousin's hand.

"You REALLY need to come back home. I don't know what you're doing, but we can figure it out if you're here. I can't help you if you're far away"

"But I have court…"

"Baby, if you're HERE, I can help you. Come home."

"But…"

"Let me help you. Please? Please come back."

And just like the other idiots in his fucking family, he bought it and said he was on his way. Later that evening he made it back and the "talk" commenced. I honestly have NO idea what we talked about, at all. Not one clue. Except for one phrase uttered from his lips, "I can't love you like you want to be loved." Love me? LOVE ME ? Fuck, you don't have any regard for me at ALL, you arrogant fucking self-centered douche bag! WhatEVER. You fucking ABANDONED ME IN THE MIDDLE OF NOWHERE FUCKING KENTUCKY!!!!!

Okay, so after we had the "talk" and after it was all said and done, he convinced me I was still obligated to help him with his restitution, so like a totally stupid, co-dependent, weak, abused, obedient woman, I gave him the $1000 to pay his fines. That grand exchange was then followed up with a conversation with Van-boy's stepsister, who proceeded to tell me what a total dickhead he was. DUH! Oh, and how the ENTIRE time he had been fucking his cousin's little girlfriend's LITTLE SISTER! She couldn't have been over fifteen. SICK! GROSS! CHILD MOLESTER!

That's when I lost it. Not that he was fucking a child, but that I had been so completely, utterly, and totally betrayed. Yet, I was so damned blind to it. As if being left in the middle of nowhere at some hick gas station wasn't enough, but being cheated on and lied to somehow was the catalyst that sent me over the edge. Huh. My naiveté was pretty pathetic, but wait! It gets even MORE pathetic!

So, I left. I drove to a gas station a few miles away, bought two boxes of sleeping pills, some blue juice, and holed up in my van. I put a note on the window, just in case he came looking for me. It said that I needed time to think and I would be okay in the morning. They came...and they knocked...and I remained silent...and they left. I opened the pills and made one big pile. AGAIN, I said, "here goes nothing," just like I had done three years earlier, but unlike when I was sixteen, this time I was afraid. Because of that, because I knew it was the wrong thing to do, my body rejected those stupid little pills. FAST. I took four or five small handfuls. And decided to smoke one last cigarette before I finished. Just as I was about to light up, without any warning, I puked all those little pills up. Every single one of them. All over the inside of my van. Blue juice and pills. EVERYWHERE. Now, here's the thing. Enough of the pills had absorbed into my bloodstream that I was high as FUCK and terrified. I didn't want to die, and I didn't know what else to do. The one person that had known me for years that had been claiming to love me had abandoned me ENTIRELY. I had nobody. I had nothing. My bridges were ashes and I didn't know what else to do. Suicide got me everything I wanted the last time I tried it, so why the fuck wouldn't it work again? It didn't. Not even close.

I managed to stumble out of the van, call Van-boy's house, and whisper to his brother, "I did something very bad and I need help. Please come get me." It sounded like I was in a tunnel in a dream. The words were barely audible out of my mouth, even in my own head. I have no idea how he heard me. It was not even a whisper. It was like words floated along on my breath, and only if you were paying close attention would you catch them. Somehow he did.

I don't remember anything until a few hours later. I was lying on the floor in Van-boy's mother's house, under a table. I kept imagining Van-boy coming over to check on me, hovering over me like a demon waiting for his prey to come alive so he could kill it. Then he'd retreat and then he'd come back and then he'd retreat. I have no idea if it was real or just a stupid hallucination, but it felt like I was lying at the gates of hell and he was waiting for me to die to bring me in.

I remember writhing in agony, crying and screaming in pain. I recall crawling to the bathroom to throw up and slithering back to my lowly place beneath the table. He'd come back to me and then he'd retreat. Then he'd come back to me and then retreat, again. Like a reptile I'd slither to the bathroom to throw up. ALL night like that. Over and over.

Finally morning came. And for the second time, I wasn't dead.

I had three choices of where I could go: I could go to Chicago, I could go to California, or I could go to Virginia. Chicago was where my family was, but they had kicked me out before I left for my first Dead tour, so that was out. California is where I wanted to be, but I was scared of driving the van 3,000 miles. So, that was out.   The only option left was good old Virginia! Great.

I decided to ask Van-boy for my money before I left. Guess what he said! You guessed it! He said no! Then he laughed and added, "Megan, I have a house full of people that would vouch for me that you GAVE me the money.   There is NOTHING you can do."   I suppose I had underestimated the idiot because he was right and I simply didn't have much fight left in me. So I left. I walked across that yard, my back to Van-boy and his brother, feeling their eyes bore into me, laughing at me, mocking me. It was a walk of shame and I was humiliated. GOD DAMN IT!

I climbed up into the van and headed east. I was hysterical. My life, as I had known it, was over. The one person that was supposed to love me no matter what and that knew me better than anyone else, didn't want anything to do with me. I felt like a fucking leper. I sobbed and screamed and cursed and drove.

As I've mentioned, the van was a total hunk of shit and it was very difficult to drive. The front end was all fucked up and I had to move the steering wheel like I was driving a boat. Big, sweeping motions – right hand at 12:00 then at 3:00 then over to 9:00 then back to 12:00. And I still couldn't keep the fucker in one lane. So at 8:00 in the morning, I got pulled over for a DUI. At EIGHT A.M.!!! The state trooper did the standard test: "Walk the line, ma'am. Touch your nose, ma'am." He listened to me sob and explain my story "it's the van...I SWEAR!" and he decided to take pity on me. (Poor thing got left at a gas station...huh...) He called a service station a few exits away and made sure that they could see me that day, so I could at least drive somewhat safely through his state. He also told all the other troopers to leave me alone, and let me get to where I was going. While I was happy for some help, I was secretly hoping he'd find the small amount of pot Van-boy left in the icebox. (Again, what's with the icebox?) Part of me wanted to be arrested. I would have a place to sleep, food to eat, and I wouldn't have to drive my big, cool, scary hippy-van anymore. Unfortunately, he didn't find it and I was still on my own, all alone. So off I went, down the road, to the service station, where they did what they could to stabilize my front end, and I was on my way again. This time the van was slightly steadier than it had been, and so was I. There was something about having someone, anyone, care enough about me to find me a service station. Granted, I was a danger to every single other vehicle on the road, even those people just thinking about driving, but it still made me feel a little less alone. It was as if maybe someone did care, even if it was just a little bit.

Now, Virginia is a pretty long way from Kentucky and in a van that won't go over fifty, it's even farther. As I was plugging along, I got to a point in West Virginia where I realized three things. First, they were doing construction on the highway and I was in the only open lane. Second, I was the front car in a LONG line of cars in this lane. Third, the car behind me was close...VERY close. And he had a blue light on his dashboard. It wasn't spinning or anything, but it was there, nonetheless. FUCK. GREAT. I was white knuckled already, doing everything in my power to keep that stupid van in the stupid lane. Now I've got some police-type person literally driving up my ass. FUCK. I did NOT want to get pulled over again. I just wanted to get to fucking Virginia. FUCK. Fine, stupid West Virginia. I'll get off at the next exit I see. Thank GOD it was a rest area. I put on my blinker and started moving the van off the highway. The car behind me blitzed past me as fast as he possibly could, only inches from my van. He went so fast that I was literally almost knocked off the road, but I didn't care. I needed to smoke a cigarette and to walk around for a minute to compose myself. I had my eye on the prize and nothing was gonna stop me.

As I started rolling into the rest area, I pushed on my brake to slow down, but nothing happened. So, I pushed again. Nothing. I started to pump it. Nothing. I pulled myself up by my steering wheel and put every single ounce of weight I had on it. NOTHING! I was driving WAY too fast into a parking lot with people and cars and I COULD NOT STOP. So, I whipped it into a spot, let the van roll up onto the curb, threw it into reverse, let it roll back down, threw it in park, turned it off, and started laughing. WHAT THE FUCK! LOL! OH MY GOD. What the fuck was I supposed to do now? I was nowhere near my destination and I was stuck. REALLY stuck. So, I did the only thing I could do. I got out of the van, lit a cigarette, and walked over to the pay phone to start making phone calls. My friend in Virginia said she would totally come get me, but being the stubborn girl that I was, I said that I would figure it out.

As I was walking back to my van, I started laughing, and a number of men in business suits asked me if I was okay. Here was this little hippy girl, bare feet, long skirt, Guatemalan shirt, and long dark hair back in a bandana, laughing. Just walking and laughing. I just smiled at each of them and said, "I'm fine, thank you."

I got back to my van and this guy came up to me and asked me if I was okay. He then said that he had witnessed what that federal agent did to me, riding my ass and nearly running me off the road, because he had been right behind him. **FEDERAL AGENT???** He asked me if I was going to press charges and I explained that I was just passing through on my way to Virginia, but my van lost its brakes. He said that he had a van just like mine at home and that maybe he could help me. So, I popped the hood and in he went.

After a few minutes, he called me over, dipped his fingers into some container on the passenger side of my van's engine, held his fingers out, and said, "Smell." As I brought my nose closer, the smell of pure alcohol was potent, becoming even more so as my nose got closer. He then asked me if I knew what happened when someone put alcohol in the brake reservoir of a vehicle. Wait, someone PUT alcohol in my van? Of course I didn't know. "It corrodes the line and you lose your brakes." Huh…Van-boy. HE did it. Huh...Van-boy had tried to kill me. GREAT. Fucking GREAT. He couldn't get rid of me by abandoning me in the middle of nowhere, so he tried to kill me. Fucking awesome...

As we were standing there talking about how I was almost murdered, a creepy motorcycle guy pulled into the rest area. I kept thinking over and over, "Please don't come over here. Please don't come over here. Please don't come over here." And almost as if he heard me and wanted to spite me, over he came. The two men started talking about the situation, and decided that if they bled the line and got the van back to the first guy's house, they could fix it. What else was I supposed to do? I was a girl, all alone, with almost no money. I had no choice, but to trust two total strangers, in the middle of West Virginia. So, I climbed into the first guy's car and off we went to get the supplies.

From the moment I got into his car, I got this funny feeling, like something wasn't quite right. He kept looking at me, hard, in a way that made me very uncomfortable. I knew I was in trouble and all I wanted was to get away from him as fast as I could, but FUCK, he was helping me! Right? RIGHT??? I got the brake fluid while he got a beer and when we got back into the car, he cracked the can open and rested it between his legs and up against his "maleness". I was sick. I was scared. I was totally trapped and he knew it. Why he didn't pull off the road and rape me right then I will never know.

We got back to the van, the boys did their mechanic stuff, and told me to get in and follow them to the guy's house. WHAT! DRIVE MY VAN THAT ALMOST KILLED ME??? Oh my GOD!!! We were only going a few miles and they said that they would make sure I was safe. So I climbed in, terrified, knowing that the last time I drove the death trap, it I had no brakes. We drove sssllllloooooooowwwwwlllllyyy and, somehow, made it to his trailer. It was on what seemed like a pretty decent sized piece of property (lots of room to hide the bodies?). I parked the van. Bob, the creepy motorcycle guy, parked the bike, and up into the house we all went. As soon as we walked in, the phone rang and the guy picked it up. Bob and I were talking about nothing, and I suddenly realized I could hear a woman screaming through the phone. The conversation didn't last very long, but when the guy got off, he said his girlfriend was pissed that there was another woman in the house, she heard me laughing and talking, and we'd have to sleep outside.

Uh, okaaayyyyy...

So, Bob pitched his tent, I climbed into my van, and to sleep we went.

The next morning, I heard a knock on my door. Bob the motorcycle guy was standing outside, with a cup of coffee for me and said, "Good morning sunshine! I brought you some coffee. Oh and here's a note the guy left."

"Megan, I don't have the parts. I can't help you. Tell Bob it's gonna rain."

Uh, okaaayyyyy…

In response to the bewildered look on my face, Bob said, "I think you should drink your coffee and go across the street and get cleaned up in their bathroom. I'll drive down the road a ways to find a service station that will take us today."

Uh, okaaayyyyy…

After about 30 minutes, he came back to the van and said that he had found one a few miles away. Away we went. We spent all day there. Bob went out and got us stuff for sandwiches and stuff to drink. Whatever I wanted. He waited and waited and waited with me, all day and he promised me that even if he had to go buy another helmet, he would make sure I safely reached Virginia, even if it was on the back of his bike.

The creepy motorcycle guy turned out to be my leather-wearing, Harley-riding guardian angel.

At nearly sunset, the mechanics said it was as good as it was going to get, and we could take it away. Bob asked me if I was okay to drive it, but what choice did I have? ZERO. So, yes, I'm fine. I climbed in and start following him. As we were curling through the Appalachians, I noticed a sign that read "7% grades up ahead." Ummmmm….WHAT! I was just a few miles from hitting SEVEN PERCENT GRADES ON A MOUNTAIN ROAD WITH NO FUCKING BRAKES!!!!! I was nearly a dead person. THANKS A LOT VAN-BOY!!! A few more miles, and I mean just a few. Had that Fed not been driving up my fucking ass, I would NOT have pulled over, I would have hit those grades and I would have had NO CHANCE! HOLY SHIT!!! I tried to focus on my driving, and on controlling the unruly van, but I couldn't get that grade sign out of my head. OH, MY FUCKING GOD!!!

Somehow, we finally got through the mountains and came to a truck stop. Now, this wasn't just any truck stop. This was by far the coolest, nicest, most incredible truck stop EVER. It even had showers! Not just regular showers, but huge, elephant-power, hot, hot showers! It was the best shower I've EVER had and since I had been on the road for a while, one I sorely needed. Then we had dinner at a truck-stop pizza place and got ready for bed. I told him that he could sleep in the van with me. I mean, he had pretty much saved my life and I figured a night off the pavement and out of the tent was the least I could do.

We climbed in and sat up talking and smoking the little bit of pot that Van-boy had left as a departing gift. I found out that Bob didn't know why he stopped at that rest area. He didn't need to go to the bathroom. He wasn't tired. The bike wasn't acting up. He just felt compelled to do so. We both knew that, if he hadn't stopped, I would have ended up a rape victim at best, a murder statistic at the worst.

The next morning we parted ways. We were nearly in Virginia and I had about a half day of driving left. Bob felt certain I would make it safely, and he needed to head home. I've never heard from him again, but I always imagined that if I HAD called the number he gave me, a lady would answer the phone and say, "Bob? Oh honey, he was killed years ago in a horrible motorcycle accident on I-64 in West Virginia." I liked the mystery. I liked the fantasy. I liked believing that he came back to save me. ME. I WAS worth it and I deserved it.

I didn't hear from Van-boy again either…until sixteen years later. I saw him on Facebook. I sent him a message. We chatted. I realized he was completely anti-social, totally boring, and nothing more to me than a huge obstacle dumped in my path, for YEARS. He didn't deny trying to kill me but he didn't accept responsibility for it either. He didn't pay me my money. He showed no signs of growth or change or maturing. But he did share a story with me. A few years earlier, he had gotten an infection in his mouth, which somehow went into his heart, which then proceeded to get really sick and caused him to lose his leg. I believed him because I saw a picture of his prosthetic leg! I've never seen karma act so quickly nor have I ever really SEEN it in my own lifetime. Yet, there it was. A disease in his heart caused him to lose a leg! A heart smaller than that of the Grinch caused him to lose his leg! I deleted him off my page a few weeks later...

And so the contemplation begins...

Not a lot to say on this one. Except...

MORAL: When desperation is confused with love, we are willing to overlook the obvious.

Chapter 6

MY FATHER HAS CANCER

And so the story begins...

I was a grown-up. I had moved all the way to California to start my grown-up life (and to see some more Dead shows...let's be honest). And I had repaired my relationship with my father. And we were best friends.

One day, the phone rang. It was my dad. "Meg, I have cancer." I dropped the phone like it had just caught fire. I stood motionless. Seconds passed. I was numb. I picked up the phone and muttered, "I'm gonna have to call you back." I hung up and began to sob and sob and sob. I only stopped when I realized it was not helping, I was not helping. I picked up the phone and dialed my parents' number. I talked to my dying father.

He was diagnosed with colon cancer and would be having it removed in a few weeks. I said I was quitting school and that I was coming home. He said no. He said "stay in school." He said he'd be fine, but I knew he wouldn't.

I hung up the phone. I took a shower and when I got out, my friends were there. We got high. I felt better.
~~~~~~~~~~~~~~~~~~~~~~~~~~~~~~~~~~~~
My father and I talked, at least weekly, while we waited for operation day. The Saturday

before surgery, we had a long conversation about nothing. We talked about mutual funds. We talked about school. We talked about snow and we talked about rain. He and I were really good at that...talking about nothing. It was often more like we were pals than father/daughter. Unless, of course, there was something I needed a father's advice on. Then he did the best he could to help me find my way.

But the Sunday night before surgery, I got this strange feeling. My mother would say "a ghost had walked across my grave." I decided that I needed to talk to him, to tell him just one more time before surgery that I loved him. I picked up the phone. I slowly dialed my parents' number. As he answered, I choked back my tears and said "Daddy, I just wanted to tell you that I love you." It was the last time I ever talked to him as the man I knew.

Surgery day came and along with the surgery came dementia - surgery induced dementia or Anoxia to be precise. It is basically like immediate-onset Alzheimer's and he would never, ever, ever be the same. He would struggle with time and place. He would struggle with who people were and how they fit into his life. He would struggle with who he was and how he fit into his life. He would struggle with his past as if it was his present. All of his demons were alive, well, and terribly vocal. He was in his own private living hell while I got to watch as a helpless bystander.

He had forbidden me to leave school to come home while he was sick, and made me promise that I would finish the semester. So, I stayed in California while he deteriorated in Chicago. My mother told me that he never talked about any of the children except for me and that I was the only child he ever called, or even ever talked about calling while he was dying. I was the only friend he had. He and my mother hated each other, and while she put on a fabulous "almost a widow" demeanor, it was mostly driven by her desire to play the role. She was always good at that...role-playing. Oh, and she was such a good widow. As a matter of fact, her friends had to tell her to stop wearing all black and going to his grave nearly a year after his death. I think she was acting out the final scene of her horrific and abusive treatment of him. They tortured each other for years in a loveless marriage, full of passive-aggressive comments said under each other's breath, just loud enough to be heard. I can say this because I watched it. My siblings were all long gone, out of the house, as I watched my mother transform from an attentive and subservient housewife into a "liberated" woman. It was as if when she went back to work, she realized that she didn't need to put up with the domestic expectations of the 1950's. She was angry. She was bitter and she hated him for the prison he locked her in. The fucked up thing is that it was a prison she signed up for. Fuck...this book is as much for her as it is for anyone. Funny how that works out. Almost a shame that she'll never be able to hear what I am saying. This is where I break into tears.

My family. My mother, my siblings...all of them warned me that my father probably wouldn't remember me when I went to visit him after the semester was over. So when we got to the hospital, I tentatively walked into his room, almost tiptoeing. I was afraid he wouldn't know me. I was afraid they'd be right. Somehow, they liked that. They liked that I always thought they knew better than I did. Even though I was afraid, even though THEIR voices were louder in my head than my own, I instinctively knew, deep where all the real truths lie, that he would know me. He was my father and he loved me. So I cautiously approached his bed, which was surrounded by a bunch of people I didn't know. "Hi Daddy." And he immediately and enthusiastically said, "Megan Anne!" My Daddy knew who I was. He knew EXACTLY who I was. I was more than relieved. I was elated. FUCK those people that doubted us!

Over the next two weeks, I saw him nearly every day. I sat with him. I held his hand. I watched people talk about him like he wasn't there. We rolled our eyes at each other. I told him stories. I listened to his stories. At one point, he got stuck and couldn't remember what he was trying to tell me. I said, "it's okay, Daddy, take your time." He looked at me with the saddest eyes I had ever seen and quietly said, "It's not about time anymore, Meg." That's when I knew he knew he was dying and that's when my heart splintered into a million shards of sorrow. I knew I was going to lose my best friend and my only ally in my family. I knew I was going to be alone.

Prior to this trip to visit my father, I had the bright idea to do a family portrait. It was the first and only time that all of his children and grandchildren would be together. So it seemed like a good idea to capture the moment. My sister, the alpha of the siblings and only local child, coordinated a photographer to come to the extended care facility that had been our father's home for nearly six months. We had the tiniest of windows of time – only a few hours when we'd all be together, but we were going to make this work.

Instead, something happened that day. My father had vanished. He had, at last, retreated to the deepest recesses of his mind, his heart, and his soul. He was simply not there. He was vacant. His body had become a shell of the man that once was. He didn't speak. He made weird, uncomfortable eye contact, as if he was looking right through you like you were just a ghost. Because that is what he had become...a ghost. He was a shadow that was taking breath in unison with his family. He had this weird, awkward grin on his face. I am not even sure how to describe it, really. It was almost a grimace. It was kind of like he knew a secret and wasn't gonna tell anyone. He looked bitter, kind of angry, and annoyed at the whole scene that lay before him. Here was his family, a group of people, most of whom barely knew each other. Yet, here we all were. His brood. Standing and kneeling around him like his subjects. King for a day, at last. We were there to honor him and he knew it was all bullshit. The photo wasn't for him. We weren't there for him. We were there for us. People become extremely selfish when someone is dying. They don't care about the person in the bed or in the wheelchair. All of their actions are driven by self preservation masked with concern and grief for the pending loss of another life, but it's all a fucking joke. A tightrope walk of thin bloodlines. He didn't want that fucking picture taken. He would have been humiliated by it. HUMILIATED.

I had fallen into the herd mentality and thought that this brainchild of an idea of mine was marvelous. I was so excited to see the whole fake family together. But after I took one look at the photographs, I realized it was a mistake and that this would be the last image I had of him...only it wasn't him. He was in a wheelchair. He was in a gray fleece sweatshirt, which I still wear from time to time. He looked more like a prop than the patriarch of the family. It was staged. It was a play. It was the final scene in, "We really ARE a good family." Somehow, I had unintentionally

written the entire final act. I felt sick.
~~~~~~~~~~~~~~~~~~~~~~~~~~~~~~~~~~~~~

I had been back in California for a few
weeks when my sister's voice came across on the
answering machine at about 5 am. She didn't say
anything other than I needed to call her
immediately, but when I did, all I got was her
voice mail. So, I went to work, already knowing
in my heart what she was going to tell me. I
waited for nearly four hours to hear from her.
FOUR HOURS. While four hours may not seem
that long, it's an eternity when you are just
waiting to hear the most heart-breaking news
ever. It was the longest block of time in my life. I
couldn't believe she made me wait so long. WHO
THE FUCK leaves a message like that on an
answering machine when someone's dying and
makes the recipient wait four hours for a callback?
FINALLY, she called me and said, "Meg, Daddy
died. I've got you a flight for tomorrow morning."
I closed my office door, finished up a few loose
ends and quietly snuck down the hall into my
boss' office, burst into tears and left by way of the
back door. I didn't want anyone to know. I didn't
want to hear the pity. I didn't want the hugs. I
wanted to run away from, well, everything. I
wanted to be invisible with my pain. I wanted to
be alone with my pain. I wanted to be away from
the sorrow others would feel for me. Because
whatever grief and sadness they might feel, it was
nothing compared to the hole that had just been

ripped through my already shredded heart. My father was dead and I was alone.

My first night in Chicago after my father died, my mother, my sisters, my brother, X and I were all sitting on my parents' porch, discussing the funeral. My mother wanted each of us to participate in some way. My siblings were each to do a reading at the funeral (I think), and since I was the poet in the family, she wanted me to recite a poem. I told her no, that it would be too hard for me to do. I knew what would happen. I knew I would lose it in front of everyone, but my oh-so-delightful siblings said that I had to "because it's what Mom wants." So I begrudgingly agreed, all the while waiting for the moment of my unavoidable and very public tear-shed.

The night of the wake (that's how Roman Catholics roll), I saw lots of family and friends that I hadn't seen in a very long time. It was very surreal. Why does death bring people together like that? People I hadn't seen in years, all hugging and caring and consoling. So mandatory. So fake and so very phony.

After the events of the evening, I remember lying on a sofa on the opposite side of the room from where my father lay quietly in his coffin. I was pretending I was lying with him, which is weird because we never ever snuggled like that, except for THAT night. We were the only two people in the room, and I felt oddly close to him. He was my father. He was my friend. He was my confidant. He was the only familial support I had as an adult...and he was in the fucking box. FUCK. It was the last time I was ever alone with him. A 27-year old should not have to bury her father.

The next day we all gathered once again at the funeral home. Members of the audience that knew I had to read a poem made bets to see how far I would make it through the short piece before I lost it. When my turn came, I stood up, walked to the front of the room, took a breath, and began to read a poem from some unknown author.

> God looked around his garden
> And He found an empty place.
> He then looked down upon this earth,
> And saw your tired face.
> He put his arms around you
> And lifted you to rest
> God's garden must be beautiful
> He always takes the best.
> He knew that you were suffering
> He knew that you were in pain
> He knew that you would never
> Get well on earth again.
> He saw that the road was getting rough,
> And the hills are hard to climb.
> So He closed your weary eyelids,
> And whispered, "Peace be thine."
> It broke our hearts to lose you
> But you didn't go alone
> For part of us went with you
> The day God called you home.

I got through nearly the entire piece, reading as quickly as I could while trying to make sure I was comprehensible. Then at the last four lines, something inside me snapped and I exploded into a storm of hysterical tears. I heard a few muffled sobs from the audience as I stood up in front this room full of people with my tortured heart and my love for my father on display. I couldn't move. I don't think I took a breath. All I could do was cry. And cry. And cry. There was no closing the floodgates this time and do you know who came up to console me? My mother? One of my siblings? My childhood best friend? NO! THE FUCKING FUNERAL DIRECTOR!!!!!!! She came up, wrapped her arms around me, and held me while I wept, as if I was her own, spilling my grief and my pain on her shoulder. After what seemed an eternity, she slowly walked me back to my seat between my sister and my mother. Still sobbing and still needing to be consoled, I put my head on my sister's shoulder for a few moments. I don't even remember if she hugged me or touched me or even just leaned into me a little bit. It doesn't really matter. The only reason she was the one beside me was because that's how we ended up. Not because we were close or even somewhat friends. Just two people that happened to be born into the same fucked up family.

At the end of the ceremony, right before they carried my father to the hearse, everyone went up to say their final goodbyes. As his immediate family, we were last. My sisters, my nieces, and my mother all stood together. My brother, his wife, and X stood together. I stood alone because the person that would have been beside me was in the box. HE WAS IN THE BOX!!!...and my heart was in there with him. Forget breaking. I was broken.

They then escorted us into a private waiting room while my father was carried from the building. I sat, weeping and moaning. Breathing had become an effort. Talking was impossible. I just sat there, alone, trembling, aching, sorrowful, pitiful. My mother put her hand tightly on my shoulder and said, "Megan Anne, KNOCK IT OFF." A slap could not have hurt as much. I sat, stunned. In all of three seconds I went from a sobbing pile of emotional wreckage to a hard, cold rock that had just happened to have lost her father. My mother could not tolerate such a display of true feelings. She never liked it when I was outwardly emotional, which is pretty fucked up seeing as how I have always worn my emotions on my sleeve. I can't lie. I can't pretend. When I'm hurting, the whole world always knows - clear as the ice that flowed through my mother's existence.

Later that night, my sisters and I were sitting in my childhood bedroom, talking about our relationships with our father. One of them said to me, "You know Meg, the only reason Daddy was nice to you was because you were his last chance at being a good father." Ummmmm…EXCUSE ME???? I gritted my teeth and calmly responded, "Did you ever consider the fact that maybe he was nice to me because I was nice to him?" They both thought for a second and then shook their heads. "No, it was because you were his last chance." Ummmmmm…EXCUSE ME??? You hated him. HATED HIM!!! Just as our mother had trained us. You could not see the man for who he was but only as the evil, thoughtless, mean image that she had created. It was an act. It was a game. It was a fabrication. She could not handle anyone liking him more than her and she did everything in her power to ensure that it would not, could not ever happen. Only it did. It happened with me. We all warned our boyfriends that our dad was tough but our mother was easy as pie and every boyfriend I've ever brought home asked if I had been kidding. Our mother never failed to say nasty, hurtful things to these poor boys, while our father just sort of sat there, invisible. I was trained, conditioned, to believe that my mother was the nice one and my father was the monster.

The day after we put my father in the ground, my mother, my sister, and I were sitting in the living room. My mother was sitting in my father's gold recliner. My sister was sitting in the gold armchair. I was sitting on the gold and tan love seat. The vast sea of green grass-colored carpet lay between us. Somewhere in the middle of the tranquility and casual conversation in my parents' green and gold living room, something in my mother snapped and she launched into a tirade of exquisite and specific verbal abuse. She proceeded to tell me what a horrible daughter I had been and how my father had always resented me for talking to him about his diabetes. How I was, in general, a disappointment. She went on and on and on. Only, I had stopped listening. Her words were drowned out by my internal screams and sobs and by the silence of my sister, who sat there spineless, wordless, failing to defend her baby sister. I was alone in a barrage of verbal attacks that were sharper than any blade that could possibly cut my flesh. My mother was a Cuisinart and I was a tomato being crushed into a red, lifeless, gooey puree.

I had been a BAD daughter? He had ALWAYS resented me? I didn't understand. It made no sense to me. I was the ONLY one he talked to on the phone every week before surgery. I was the ONLY one he talked to after surgery. I was the ONLY one he shared things with. THE ONLY ONE. ARGHHHHHHHHHHHH!!! How could she even begin to say such things to me at all, never mind just days after his death? I ran upstairs to my bedroom, hysterical, sobbing out of control, shaking to the core of my being. WHY was she so hurtful, so spiteful, so mean? Why did she hate me so much? WHY???????

A few minutes later my mother came in

and calmly asked me what was the matter, as if the previous ten minutes hadn't just happened. It was as if she had no recollection of the attack she had just assaulted me with, no idea where my damage had come from, no clue that she was somehow the catalyst for the watershed flowing from my eyes. There was no recognition of the pain she had just inflicted on me. If there was any recognition, it seemed more like she had accomplished her jealous goal...to hurt me; to cause me pain. Actually, now, more than ten years later, I swear I can SEE her with an evil, sneaky grin curling around the corners of her mouth as she asked me what was wrong, as if she was pleased with the situation, pleased with the pain she had inflicted, like she was happy but trying to hide it. Now, maybe I'm just imagining this or maybe my bitterness is allowing me to remember things that might not have been real at the time, but as I reflect back on this, that "grin" has ALWAYS bothered me. But I've never really admitted to having seen it. Until TODAY. I saw it. I believe it. She had meant to hurt me. BADLY. And she did. I went months without speaking to her because of it, but per the norm, I allowed her back in, just to cause some more damage. She was the person I called when I was having a stupendous day. Every time. Why? Partly, because secretly, deep down, I always hoped that she would be proud of me, maybe even to be happy for me. It was also because she would always be the one to bring me back down, to regress me back to the girl that was never good enough. NEVER. I knew she would make sure I remembered this. It was the message I had been trained to live by, and when I wasn't doing so, I needed her to teach it to me again.

The night before I left Chicago, my mother and sisters decided to have a "girls' night". My father's sister came with us. I sat quietly, listening, observing, watching the women in my family of origin. I watched my niece desperately try to get her mother's attention, only to be yelled at. I saw the look of disappointment and sadness ringing through her face. Pure loneliness. I knew all too well what that felt like and I wanted to tell her, to hug her, to make sure she knew she was loved and adored, because I knew that was what she wanted. Christ. That's all I had ever wanted, but I knew that any sort of acknowledgement would simply escalate into something I had no desire to deal with. How dare I intervene in the upbringing of my niece? How dare I confront her mother, my sister, the perfect Miss Wonderful? Who the fuck was I to speak up? Oh, wait, I know. I was no one. I was the mistake. I was the youngest. I was the embarrassment. So, I just sat by and let my beautiful, sweet little niece just sit there, swimming in her own misery, all alone. She was just a little girl looking for love from the one person that should always be willing to give it. I did nothing and I hated myself for it. I just sat there as my sister had during my mother's verbal diarrhea the day before. I will never forgive myself for that, for being afraid to say what I thought, for failing to protect that perfect, precious little girl. I asked my niece about this years later. And thankfully she does not remember.

~~~~~~~~~~~~~~~~~~~~~~~~~~~~~~~~~~~

As we were leaving the restaurant, my aunt pulled me aside, away from the other women. She wanted to tell me just how proud my father was of me, how much he loved me, and how the best day of his life was the day he walked me down the aisle. While deep in my heart and soul, I knew all of this was true, it was still so reassuring to hear it from someone that knew him, and knew him well. He DID love me. He WAS proud of me. He WAS glad I existed. I was his daughter. I was his friend. I was his confidant and I would miss him forever, because without him, I had no real family.

And the contemplation begins...

Wow...I don't really even know what to say. Except that today is Father's Day and I miss my dad.

MORAL: If you ever feel the need to tell someone you love them, don't be afraid. Shout it at the top of your lungs from the highest mountain because it may be the last time you get the chance to.

Chapter 7

OPIATE ADDICTION – ROUND ONE

And so the story begins...

I had toured with the Dead in my early twenties, so I was no stranger to drugs. Even before I went on tour, I had always had a fascination with heroin. I remember my friend Onion and I were eighteen years old and ready to try it. We had a connection that we more or less trusted, but it just never panned out. Then, one day, I was sitting with one of my girlfriends, and my friend B said, "So, you guys wanna get some heroin?" She and I looked at each other, smirked, and said, "Yeah, right!" He swore he could get it, and so we finally said yes, partly to see if he could do it, and partly to see if we would do it. So, he left to score. She and I sat there, sort of dumbfounded, not sure if we were willing to believe what was about to happen, but happen it did.

He came home with a chunk of sticky, black tar and dropped it into a liquid herb bottle, the brown kind with the pipette. We waited about fifteen minutes for it to dilute. I was excited and nervous, all at the same time. I was about to try something that I had wanted to try for YEARS, but had never had the chance to. But I also knew it was something that could take over my life completely and kill me easily. At the time, I didn't really care….

B lay back across the couch, dropped his head back over the arm, and shot a pipette full of that brown liquid straight up his nose. The nervous anxiety was nearly too much and my friend and I were both stupid-excited and I let her go next. She assumed the same position that he had, only he dropped the brown liquid into her nose for her. She scrunched up her face like she had just smelled the most disgusting thing EVER, grabbed her nose, sat up on the couch and made a sound like she wanted to puke. But the urge eventually subsided and then she just looked, well, high. REALLY, REALLY, REALLY high. The disgust on her face did nothing to dissuade me, and I was still just as giddy as a fucking kid on Christmas day. I got up on the couch, lay back, and let him get me high for the first REAL time in my life. Now, I had been strung out on all sorts of pills and powders prior, but I had never, ever been high like that. I am a chronic, perpetual, and exponential thinker and for the first time in my whole life, my brain slowed. I was floating and high and happy. When I closed my eyes, I imagined what the world would look like if on the ends of each of our fingers we had little hands with five more fingers. Oh, the sweet possibilities! I had fallen in love. This was no puppy love…this was head-over-heels, I-need-you-like-I-need-air-and-water love.

We spent hours that weekend locked in our own opiate-induced dreams. They were so visual with such an amazing body high. I felt light and airy and somehow clean, like my thoughts were clearer than ever before, like a link to a new part of my brain had just been opened up, and I was seeing things in a totally new and different way, with a new set of goggles.

B and I slowly became "weekend warriors" and our home became a local heroin den. He would make the run on Friday after work so that we, and whoever else decided to hang out with us over the weekend, would be high for three days or so. I was determined to never let it get so out of hand that we were using during the week…weekends only. We'd be ripped on Friday night, all day Saturday, all day Sunday, and then high by residual all day Monday. Tuesday we would start to feel sort of icky, like we might be coming down with the flu or something. Wednesday it became harder to sit through class and work. It was like little bugs were burrowing through each of our muscles and then Thursday would happen. While we would be in near agony, we knew that Friday would be the next day and we'd be high again. So, that made the withdrawals easier. Plus, I reasoned that if we got high all the time, then that Friday high would never be quite as fabulous. And that Friday high was ALWAYS fabulous!

Being the den mother meant I had

responsibilities to my heroin cubs. I made sure there was good water and Popsicles, for when we'd feel icky and sick, and aspirin and soda and food, just in case. We lived in the Santa Cruz Mountains in a little cabin with a big balcony. There were two big couches out front and when we would get hot and nauseated, we would lie outside in the fresh air either until the urge to puke passed or until we had to lean off the railing and barf in my front yard, leaving it there for the animals to clean up. We always had lots of music and games and activities going on inside and my cubs would slowly float around my home, all high and perfect. It was a little slice of heaven, right there in the Santa Cruz Mountains. I thought it was gonna last forever. I wanted it to. Even when a bad batch of tar came to the beach, which is where we scored, we didn't care. We knew that someone had died instantly after getting high with it because it was cut with something awful and deadly, but we needed to get high. So, we did and none of us died that weekend.

Then, B and I decided to move to Humboldt County. One of the first things I was told by one of my girlfriends was, "You guys better not bring that shit up here!" Turns out she was dating a junkie (he was clean when they hooked up) who then turned her on to the shit, got her completely hooked, and let her get arrested for growing pot...HIS pot. About eighteen months later, he died alone, in a San Francisco hotel, with a needle in his arm. He was one of my favorite people.

So, although we started out clean in Humboldt, it only lasted for about a month or so. I don't even remember who brought it around first, but there it was...and we were high. Now, I'd like to clarify one thing: I have never, ever shot it. What we did was put the tar into a bottle and dilute it with water. Then, once it was the color of watered-down cola, we'd shoot it up our noses with a pipette. It tasted like poison and the smell alone could make us puke, but after that first wave of nausea was over, the blissful, magical, floating began. I was never happier than I was after my first dropper-full, sitting outside with my dogs, smoking a cigarette. It was as if I was finally home.

When you get that high, your pupils shrink to the size of a pinhead. Now, I've got dark brown eyes that hide itty, bitty pupils really well, and I believe in maintaining a certain level of composure, so I was always able to pull it off without anyone knowing I was high. B, on the other hand, had big blue eyes with pupils that would shrink-up just thinking about heroin. So, one look at him and everyone knew. Eventually, our friends stopped coming around because our drug use made them uncomfortable. We didn't care. It just meant we could get high without the stress or fear of being scolded. We became more reclusive, with only the occasional party-goer stopping by to get high. It was usually just me and him. Of course, our stable, part-time use slowly moved into weekdays. Not all weekdays, but we started pushing it into Mondays and Tuesdays. However, thanks to my "Type-A" personality and my insanely driven motivation, I was always able to maintain some normalcy. I worked fifty hours a week at a REAL job, was taking 15-19 units per semester and graduated Summa Cum Laude, high on heroin, among other things, most of the time. Some of my best papers were written when I was blasted out of my mind on crystal meth, the complete other side of the drug spectrum. I would stay up for DAYS, write my paper, hate it, literally cut it apart paragraph by paragraph, lay it on the floor, redesign it, then retype the whole thing. A+ every time.

~~~~~~~~~~~~~~~~~~~~~~~~~~~~~~~~~~~~

One summery Friday afternoon at work, I got a call from a friend. She was calling to invite me to a memorial service for her boyfriend, who happened to be a very dear friend (wait, WHAT! Memorial service?!?!?!). We all thought that he had been clean for months when he went to visit his parents in Southern California. His mother found him on the bathroom floor with a needle hanging from his arm. I still miss him every day. I even hang my toilet paper so it's like a waterfall, because that's how he liked it. From what I can remember, we stopped getting high for a few weeks, and we put a bumper sticker on our car that said, "Heroin sucks." But we got scared that someone would think that WE were doing it so we pulled it off. Our sobriety didn't last long...

~~~~~~~~~~~~~~~~~~~~~~~~~~~~~~~~~~

New Years Eve - I have NO idea what year it was, I just know we were watching South Park and it was still really new. We were sitting in the living room, low lights, low TV. Everything has to be low with pupils the size of a needle. The dogs were sleeping, and we were nodding. Nodding isn't really being awake or asleep. It's kind of like living inside a daydream. B sat up to get another dropper and he spilled half of the bottle all over the floor. My friend and I started yelling and swearing, saying everything we could think of to make him feel like a dumb ass. I mean, REALLY! KEEP YOUR SHIT TOGETHER AND DON'T SPILL THE DRUGS!!! Once we were satisfied that we had made him feel like a total and utter jerk, we both nodded back off. Then, a few minutes later, I heard a strange sound. I looked over at B, and he was breathing "funny". I called out to him, but he didn't respond. I went over to him and noticed his lips weren't pink but were slowing turning a very pale shade of blue. OH, SHIT...He was DYING! OH, MY GOD! HE WAS OVERDOSING!!! His breathing was EXTREMELY shallow and labored and I knew he was going to die. I dialed 911, and screamed into the receiver, "HE'S OD'ING!" The dispatcher asked if I knew what on. Then my world turned to slow motion…."hhhheeerrrrrroooooooooiiiinnnnnnn". I could barely believe it fell from my lips. As soon as I hung up the phone, I tied the dogs up in the yard, moved all the furniture away from the couch he was dying on to give the paramedics room to work, and hid all the drugs. The ambulance rolled up, and for some amazing reason, there was no squad car, which meant I wasn't gonna have to try to talk my way out of a narcotics possession. Hooray for small victories!

The paramedics raced in, took one look at B, pulled him to the floor, and slammed the magic Pulp-Fiction drug into an IV. Nothing. So they did it again. The moment it hit his vein the second time, he sat up, took a HUGE gasp of air, and projectile-vomited pink, thick, chunky liquid all over the medic. They strapped him to a gurney, asked if I was okay and told us to follow them to the hospital. I was fine, hell, I was high.

When we got home from the hospital, I hated him. Not because he nearly died in front of me or because he turned me on to something that nearly killed him and had a white-knuckled grip on me. I hated him because he ruined my ride, he ruined my heaven. I had to quit getting high because HE couldn't handle it, because HE was weak and because I was the Mama Bear. Always responsible for everything, even when I was super loaded. So, out of hatred for him, out of spite (I'll show him what a total fuck-up he really is…I won't let him get high anymore!), I burned our dealer's number, dumped the remains of the heroin down the kitchen sink, and started to clean the puke up off my rug.

We were sober, maybe four months. Then friends of ours somehow brought up the topic and asked us if we wanted to get high. At least I think this is how it happened...I'm not really sure...life was a little cloudy. And just like that, we were high again. We spent hours and hours at this couple's home, but it's all one big blur. A bunch of disconnected, disjointed memories bleeding into one another. They had two separate houses during the time we were all in Humboldt, and I celebrated my birthday in one of them. I can't remember which. It's almost as if I've simply constructed them into a single memory of heroin-induced intoxication, and the details just don't really matter.

Even with all the drugs and parties, I graduated from college with high honors and B and I decided to relocate to Southern California. For whatever reason, I left heroin in Humboldt county. No regrets. No sadness. I was just done. I guess I figured that since school was over and my "real" life was about to begin and I wanted to be successful, I should probably be fucking sober...or at least not an active junkie.

B, however, did not subscribe to this theory. He OD'd one more time, only I had NO idea he was high. I had taken our friend's little girl out to get dinner and when we got home, B was sitting on the couch. His face looked sunken in, like a skeleton. His skin was pale and ashy and his eyes looked hollow, even though they were closed. He looked like he was a fucking corpse, and I didn't want the little girl to see him like that. Christ, it scared the shit outta me and I was a grown-up! I figured he would somehow become her new boogieman or something. So, I went over to him to wake him up and have him lie down. But when I got there, the little girl was right beside me, giggling. He was gurgling and bubbling out of his mouth. HERE WE GO, AGAIN!!! I called his name and started slapping his face, but nothing happened. Then I started screaming his name as loud as I could but still nothing, he was barely breathing! The little girl's dad took her outside while I was left alone to deal with the overdosing idiot in my living room. I was totally sober and truly terrified. I called 911 and told them that I didn't know what he was on, because I honestly didn't. To my knowledge, it had been years since he had touched heroin. I mean, sure, it crossed my mind, but it just didn't seem possible...or maybe I just didn't want to believe it.

The woman on the phone told me to pull him onto the ground and start administering CPR. I had never ever done it on a real person and it had been ten years since I did it on "Annie" in health class. You remember Annie, right? The mannequin with very real lips and lungs and a heart that we would practice CPR on? I remembered enough to start pushing down on his ribs. Hard. Then I'd hold his nose and push all my air into his gurgling, bubbling mouth. I watched his chest rise with every one of my exhales and fall each time I stopped blowing into his mouth. I could feel his own breath peeking through his lips, but it was ever so slight that it seemed to be trapped inside those fucking bubbles coming out of his mouth. I instantly hated him again. Not because I wasn't high too, but because he was so fucking weak.

The girl's mom came and picked her up. The paramedics took B away. The police stayed to ask questions. I walked out to my front porch to smoke a cigarette and the girl's Dad was sitting there. So I asked him, "Did you know he was high?" He paused for a second, and then whispered, "Yeah."

"YOU FUCKING KNEW AND DIDN'T TELL ME! YOU FUCKING KNEW AND DIDN'T SAY A WORD TO ME, WHILE I WAS IN THERE FUCKING SAVING HIS GOD DAMN LIFE! YOU JUST LEFT ME THERE TO DEAL WITH IT ON MY OWN WHILE YOU **KNEW!!!!!!!!!!** **GET OFF MY FUCKING PORCH!**"

"But Megan, I'm so sor..."

"I SAID **GET OFF MY FUCKING PORCH BEFORE I KILL YOU, YOU STUPID MOTHER FUCKER! YOU FUCKING KNEW!**" (Note, I am growling out loud as I write this)

I stormed back into the house followed by a

female police officer that was watching me to make sure I didn't actually strangle him. Though, I wanted to feel his life leave his body by my own, bare hands. HE KNEW! WHAT A FUCKING IDIOT! HE LET ME DEAL WITH SOMETHING THAT I KNEW NOTHING ABOUT AND DIDN'T GIVE ME THE INFORMATION I NEEDED!

I went to the hospital to pick up B's sorry ass and take him home. He never apologized, at least not until years later when he thanked me for saving his life both times. That meant more to me than he will probably ever realize. Yet, at the time of OD #2, he was actually MAD AT ME! He told me that he would have been FINE! WHAT THE FUCK DOES HE KNOW! HAS HE EVER SEEN SOMEONE BLUE-LIPPED AND DYING IN FRONT OF HIS FUCKING EYES??? **NO!!!** IT WAS ALWAYS **ME** THAT SAW IT! IT WAS ALWAYS **ME** THAT DEALT WITH IT! **AAAAAAAARRRRRRRRRRRRGGGGGGGG GGHHHHHHHHHHHHH!!!!!!!**

As we were driving home from the hospital, I told him how I almost killed his friend and he told me not to be angry with him. WHAT! NOT BE ANGRY? You are fucking RIDICULOUS!!! So, rather than continue the desire to destroy, I decided to make them understand.

His friend was staying with us at the time, and when we got home, he was hiding at the end of our driveway, not sure if he should come in or not. I called to him and invited him up to the front porch. I sat them both down and asked the friend what it felt like to watch someone almost die and to know that he could have stopped it, but didn't. I asked him if it felt good to know that if I hadn't come home when I did, hadn't reacted the way I did, that we would be at the fucking morgue preparing to bury his best friend. I asked him if he felt good about his failure to do the right thing. He was in tears. He was ashamed. He thought that by saying nothing he was protecting his friend, but really, he was giving him permission to die. They had been friends since high school, and they had been using drugs together since then, too. They had both been strung out on multiple things at different times, and keeping quiet was part of the code. The problem is that when someone is OD-ing, keeping quiet often results in someone's death.

~~~~~~~~~~~~~~~~~~~~~~~~~~~~~~~~~~~~~~~

About six months before B's final OD that included my involvement, I was in an auto accident that resulted in severe nerve damage down my right leg. I had been clean of drugs for YEARS but knew that I still had a very high tolerance. When I was put on extra strength Hydrocodone to help me with the pain, the "professionals" were not concerned about my addiction level even though they knew my history, so I wasn't either. I just wanted the pain to END and they just wanted me to be able to function. So, I ate the pills. Every day. Pill after pill after pill. Then I was put on methadone for "the management of post-spine surgery chronic pain". I got as high as I did the first time I ever tried heroin, and if I hadn't been so loaded, I would have been terrified. I even called the doctor to make sure I was okay, and he LAUGHED at me, saying that I'd get used to it in a day or so...and I did. I never got high from methadone again. It simply became a staple to manage my pain. It was a crutch to make it through the day. After eighteen months of taking at least 50 milligrams per day, I realized that I STILL had pain and that the drug wasn't serving me any longer. All I was doing was feeding this new and publicly tolerated opiate addiction. I mean, if the doctors give it to me, it must be okay. Right? RIGHT??? So, I decided to quit, just like that, and withdrew from opiates for what I'm figuring to be my very, very last time.

I'd like to add one more piece of information about the doctor that gave me the methadone...he had actually put me on so many medications that I nearly died. Literally. Every day. For months. I was on Methadone, Topiramate, Methocarbamol, Hydrocodone, Baclofen, Morphine, Diazapam, Alprazolam, Pregabalin, Lidocaine, Naproxen, and Gabapentin, in varying quantities at various times in various combinations. The largest concentration of dosing occurred at night. Now, when I began to pass out on the toilet and fall over into a pile on the bathroom floor night after night, smashing my head against the hard tile, having no idea where I was or what had happened, it didn't occur to me that the drugs were doing it. I mean, the doctor gave them to me and he IS the doctor, right? RIGHT??? And when I started having what I lovingly referred to as "broccoli" moments, the drugs never came into question. Sure, I would trail off and begin speaking in total gibberish in the middle of a conversation with the CEO or a client or a co-worker, but blame my precious drugs? NEVER! Once I began losing time almost daily, finding myself in a heap on the floor, falling asleep at the wheel in broad daylight, some of us began to think that there <u>might</u> be a problem. Did I blame my precious drugs? NEVER! So, I went to a neurologist, ready to be told I had Epilepsy or some other horrid disease. You know what he told me? He took one look at my med list, laughed and said, "You don't have epilepsy! You're overdosing EVERY SINGLE DAY!" WHAT! OVERDOSING? EVERY DAY? HOW? I'm following the prescriptions. I'M DOING WHAT I WAS TOLD!!!!! Un-fucking-believable. I was dying just a little bit every day. EVERY DAY?!?!? Who was this stupid doctor and why was he trying to destroy me? Oh wait! I know! I was referred to him by one of his childhood friends that just happened to hire me at $75k to do a $40k job only to fire me when I wouldn't, uh, respond to his "friendly" advances. I wonder if I had blown him under his desk if I would have been able to keep my job.

And so the contemplation begins…

I would like to think, to HOPE, that after watching someone almost die, or after losing a dear friend to drugs, we would stop. We would see the danger and just STOP. But it's not that easy. If the reasons for the drug abuse are NOT addressed, the user simply cannot get off. Or if they do, they substitute one thing for another. Many heroin addicts become addicted to chocolate while they are withdrawing. Similar chemicals are released, so they are just substituting. It's not the drug abuse part that's so very sad to me. It's the pain that leads into it that the addict is trying to mask. Drugs are a type of band-aid used in this quick-fix society. And until we begin to collectively search for the root cause of bad behavior, the behaviors will continue. Over and over and over and over and over again.

MORAL: The reason people fail instead of succeed is they trade what they want most for what they want in the moment. This has been said by lots of people in lots of circumstances because it's VERY true.

Chapter 8

OPIATE WITHDRAWAL –
TO END THE PAIN,
THE PAIN MUST BEGIN

And so the story begins…

While the good news is that withdrawal is possible, the bad news is that withdrawal sucks. I've read blog after blog and posting after posting about how horrible and painful it is, but I didn't believe it until I did it. Let me tell you what it was like for me…

After being on 50 milligrams of methadone for eighteen months, I decided it was time to be done. So, I started to taper at a rate that I thought was reasonable. I was cutting a 10 milligram pill in half a few times a week, dropping 5 milligrams every few days. By day six, it hurt so much that I didn't even want someone to LOOK at me. It hurt to shower, to brush my hair, to eat, to think. I hated my dogs, I hated my house, I hated my work. I hated my life. The agony in my legs was horrific. It was as if I had collected every flu ache I had EVER had and held them all right in my legs. I couldn't sleep. I was cold. I was sweaty. I wanted to die. I had to call into work with the "flu" because I knew there was NO WAY I could have sat in my cube for 8 hours. I couldn't have sat there for ten seconds! I called my doctor (not the one that started me on the methadone, but the one that had continued writing me the prescriptions and was about to help me get off the shit) and made an emergency appointment. He took one look at me and said, "You're withdrawing, aren't you?" I told him the rate of my taper and he said, "Way too fast! Go home, take your regular dose, and start a much slower taper. Five milligrams per week." WHAT! Five milligrams per WEEK??? I was shocked! I had been coming off of different drugs for years and felt fully confident in my ability to judge a taper. Five milligrams per week was going to take me two whole months! TWO MONTHS!!! But, he told me I could take some more methadone ASAP, so I was kinda happy. No, I was elated! So, as per his instructions, I went home, took twenty milligrams, and felt like a million bucks. And I felt fine for six weeks. I thought I was golden and that all the people in all the postings I had read about opiate withdrawal were big babies. Then I hit my last ten milligrams. I had always done my dose-drop on Saturdays to give me the weekend to adjust. I made it through that weekend and struggled through the workweek, alternating between wanting to kill someone or kill myself. I was unfocused, unproductive, and feeling a little guilty that I was doing this on my boss' dime.

The following Saturday I was down to my last five milligrams and I was in pure and utter agony. I was taking my dose at noon, thinking that would be as long as I could humanly possibly wait while at work. I powered through Monday and Tuesday. I cried each morning after I got out of the shower because I hurt so very, very much. It's the kind of pain and discomfort that you feel down to your soul. Every fiber hurt, every hair on my fucking head, every fingernail, every brush of the dog's tail. It felt like there were a zillion little creatures inside my body, all pulling at different pieces in all different directions, all breathing fire, all pouring acid into my muscles, drip by fucking drop. I couldn't sit still. I couldn't sleep. I couldn't think about anything but how much I hurt and how I wanted this to be over more than anything EVER. Wednesday morning, after sobbing in my bathroom, I convinced myself that I could make it. I was SOOOO fucking strong, after all. Right? RIGHT??? So, I got into my car, and drove to work. I was there for maybe two hours and realized that I wasn't even close to being done with this stupid fucking withdrawal bullshit, and that I was just gonna feel like utter and complete crap for the next two weeks at best! I still had four days of five milligrams and then the excruciating descent from five milligrams to being opiate free. I said, "Fuck this", told my boss I had the flu, and left work for the rest of the week. My last methadone dose was at noon the day before. And I was done.

I got home, ripped off my clothes, climbed into my PJs, put in a movie, and writhed and wriggled and moaned and fished and tossed in my bed for days. I would lie on a pillow, then turn over, then flip on to my back, then roll over again. I was like a fucking milkshake. And no matter what I did or how I laid, I was in utter misery. I don't remember eating anything really. I just remember taking as many non-opiate pills as I could without being afraid that I would accidentally kill myself...I'd always reserved that as my own decision. My bathroom had been a fucking pharmacy for years so I had all the supplies: Methocarbamol, Baclofen, Alprazolam, Trazodone, Hydrochloride, Promethazine, Carisoprodol, and Quetiapine, sometimes all at once. I really had no idea what the hell I was doing. I just tried to wait four hours before I took another handful of pills, but if you were to ask me today to write down what and when I took stuff, I couldn't tell you if I tried. How I didn't accidentally OD is a fucking miracle. Even the doctor said so, which was really not very comforting. And even with all those stupid pills, I still wanted to claw my legs off and kill at least three people a day. It didn't matter what three, I just wanted to see death. I had no appetite and was never thirsty. Most of my sleeping was nap-style. I would occasionally eat McDonalds, the only thing that I had even a slight taste for. Maybe, soup and toast. My house was disgusting, my bedroom was disgusting, my kitchen was disgusting, and I was disgusting. I carried a foul, near-death-type odor around with me all the time, even ten minutes after I showered. Totally fucking gross.

~~~~~~

The next five days totally blended into one another. The only distinguishing characteristic from one day to the next was that on the Friday of my withdrawal, I had to go on an interview for a part-time job at a super-swanky spa. The hilarious part was how I passed with flying colors and got the job, which was a fucking miracle. By the end of the hour-long interview, I don't think I was able to sit still for longer than ten seconds at a time. My counselor asked how I did it, how I made it through. My only response to her was that I did it because I had to, because that's what grown-ups do.

My counselor gave me three objectives during withdrawal, and they were hard enough to follow. No random sex, no killing anyone, and to get through the next thirty minutes, opiate free. I, literally, could not handle anything more than that. My judgment was totally impaired. I had no self-control, except to not touch a fucking opiate, even though I had a whole bottle in my bathroom. I called my counselor at least twice a day. She was the only positive voice inside my head that I would listen to, the only sound that reassured me; the only words that made any sense. I was erratic, confused and confusing to myself. I was all over the page, like a red ink pen that

149

exploded. Dripping with the irony and agony that was my life. I was a fucking disaster.

Then day five came... Sunday. I knew I couldn't stay home from work anymore. I knew I had to get my shit together... at least a little bit. I had no clean clothes and knew that I couldn't go to work smelling like I did. I at least needed a fresh "shell" to hide the death oozing from my body. So, I did laundry and it was HARD. I mean **REALLY** hard. The baskets were sooooo fucking heavy. And I was sooooo fucking tired. And I was sooooo fucking miserable. I just wandered through the motions, trying to remember that it would be over one day. ALL OVER.

~~~~~~~~~~~~~~~~~~~~~~~~~~~~~~~~~~

That night I went to bed, feeling more accomplished than I had in days. I was excited to sleep, but the problem was: I hadn't slept without a shit-load of pills in nearly a week and my body was still revolting from the lack of methadone. It didn't want to sleep. It didn't want to relax. It wanted to torture me. It hated me for doing this. It hated me for making it hurt so much and making me yearn for something so much. Oh, and it was going to make sure that I knew that if I ever did it again, I would have no doubt about the torture it would deliver. It was promising me pain if I ever touched an opiate again. EVER.

So I laid there. ALL NIGHT. NO SLEEP. AT ALL. NOT ONE WINK. The alarm clock went off and I nearly burst into tears. But, I got my butt up outta bed, dragged myself into the shower, and went back to work, hoping I would get struck by lightning during the entire drive in.

I made it through Monday, got home and thought for sure that I'd sleep AWESOME since I didn't sleep the night before, but I just laid there. ALL NIGHT. NO SLEEP. AT ALL. NOT ONE WINK. The alarm clock went off and, again, I nearly burst into tears. But, I got my butt up outta bed, dragged myself into the shower, and went back to work, hoping I would get struck by lightning during the entire drive in.

I made it through Tuesday, got home and thought for SURE I'd sleep AWESOME since I didn't sleep the night before. But I just laid there. ALL NIGHT. NO SLEEP. AT ALL. NOT ONE WINK. The alarm clock went off and I nearly burst into tears. But, I got my butt up outta bed, dragged myself into the shower, and went back to work, hoping I would get struck by lightning during the entire drive in.

I made it through Wednesday, got home and thought for SURE I'd sleep AWESOME since I didn't sleep the night before. But I just laid there. ALL NIGHT. NO SLEEP. AT ALL. NOT ONE WINK. The alarm clock went off and I nearly burst into tears. But, I got my butt up outta bed, dragged myself into the shower, and went back to work, hoping I would get struck by lightning during the entire drive in.

I made it through Thursday, got home and

thought for SURE I'd sleep AWESOME since I didn't sleep the night before. I finally slept for a couple of hours, but when the alarm clock went off, I nearly burst into tears. But, I got my butt up outta bed, dragged myself into the shower, and went back to work, hoping I would get struck by lightning during the entire drive in.

I made it through Friday, got home and thought for SURE I'd sleep AWESOME since I didn't sleep the night before. And FINALLY it happened. I slept. Sure, it was only for a few hours, but I slept. And the next day was Saturday. And that meant no alarm clock...

~~~~~~~~~~~~~~~~~~~~~~~~~~~~~~~~~~

I had made it eleven days without any opiates. Without killing myself. Without killing someone else. Without having random sex. And with my universe more or less intact. I had secured a new part-time job, and I had been able to keep my regular full-time job. I didn't lose my house or my dogs or my car or my mind, although there were moments when I thought one or all of them were slipping away. The reason I was on opiates in the first place was nearly forgotten. The pain in my back had simply assimilated to become such a part of me that I hardly noticed it. It was there, but it really wasn't. I would get twinges or pinches but they were simply my body talking to me. Nothing more. So I would listen, reposition it, and feel better. I would walk and walk and stretch and stretch and take LONG, hot showers.

What my body wanted, I tried to give. I wanted to make her happy in hopes that she would stop making me so fucking miserable.

After about two weeks, I still had bottles of drugs in my bathroom. My counselor asked me why, like it was a bad thing. I mean, it wasn't like I was a drug addict, right? RIGHT??? Well, when I couldn't explain to her why I still had them or why I was having an issue flushing them, I instinctively knew it was time to drown those little white bastards. I stood over the toilet, with the open bottle of methadone in my hand and the strangest thing happened. I actually started to fucking cry, like I was about to drown my best friend in the toilet. My hands started to shake and before I could talk myself out of it, I dumped the whole bottle. The street value of those little pills was hundreds of dollars. The soul value of those little fuckers was my life. I flushed every single pill I could find. All gone. No more. And my medicine chest no longer looked like a pharmacy.

I've been clean since June 20th, 2007. Today is August 1, 2007. Oh my fucking god! I had no idea it's been so long! This may not seem like much time, but after being on a "stabilizing" prescribed, socially-acceptable drug for so long and after going through withdrawals that I thought might never end, it's been nearly a lifetime. I've updated that date twice, but now I've decided to keep it where it is. I believe it's important to understand how a seemingly small

153

block of time can make all the difference in your life.

And so the contemplation begins...

INSTANT GRATIFICATION

When doing drugs, we are seeking instant gratification. It happens quickly with a pill, a puff, a snort, a plunger. It is instant. It is gratifying. It becomes our solace. It is our reward for a hard day and our escape from a crappy day. We love it because it is immediate and it is gracious. However, things that happen instantly have one substantial drawback. They have no real permanence. Look at lotto winners. Most are more broke in a few years than they were before they won. Drug addicts rarely find glowing success while using. Instead, they mask the problem, but in the end very few are able to maintain the charade long term.

In order to build long-term permanence, we must search out solutions that are NOT instant. The reason that we don't is simple. We believe it'll just take way too long to get what we want. We are impatient and we want what we want, NOW. We drive too fast, lines are too slow, and we have very little patience. However, when we are given something suddenly, it is nearly impossible to establish a lasting level of ownership. Look at sudden fame. We are not able to process the fact that the repercussions, good or bad, are our responsibility. We are looking for a quick fix to a lasting problem. Bad idea. Because, by using a quick fix, we are in essence perpetuating the problem, or at least ignoring it.

What I've realized is that all it takes is ten to fifteen minutes and the solution becomes ours. When I was withdrawing, I made it through each fifteen-minute block of time to get to the desired outcome. When I considered the long-term goal, it became overwhelming and much more difficult to see the end results, but fifteen minutes was totally doable. It was sustainable, even if I had to do it four times an hour. I've heard marathon coaches say, "the first mile ALWAYS sucks." It's a hurdle, a hump we must cross in order to get to a level of lasting gratification. It's true. Growth and change are truly a slow process. Developing ownership for our actions and for our lives is something many people work on for most of their lives. When we put it into the context of lasting and permanent change, however, the task becomes much less daunting. It falls in line with the phrase, "how do you eat an elephant?" Well, it's huge, so start simply. Start small. Start with one bite at a time. It's also the law of forward motion. Getting the car to move off a stoplight takes a considerable amount of energy. Pushing it from seventy mph to eighty mph is a gentle increase. Momentum carries us and once we engage the laws of motion, we become nearly unstoppable. All we have to do is get through those first fifteen minutes!

THE LOVE OF AN ADDICT

Love comes in so many different shapes and sizes and colors. We love our parents, we love our pets, we love our children, we love our friends. We love our cars and our homes and our laptops and our "stuff". Unfortunately, however, "love," which generally is given birth as a spiritual/mental/ emotional element, can also transition into a physical element. By this I mean it is possible to "love" something so much and become so accustomed to it, that we "need" it. When we feel a need, often there is a physical feeling of anxiety or stress if we don't have what we perceive as our need. It can make us feel sick and ill. WHAT THE FUCK AM I TRYING TO SAY HERE!!!!!!! I don't have my arms around this whatsoever.

I think what I mean is that there are many things a person can become addicted to: drugs, relationships, sex, even abuse. And the root of all of it can usually be found by asking some solid yet basic questions – who, what, where, when, why, how? They first must be asked at a superficial level, but eventually and more importantly, they must be asked at an intensely personal, spiritual, and soulful level. Otherwise, you will be trapped by a lack of acceptance of truth. An addict's natural response is "No, I'm not addicted. I'm just having a good time. I'm just partyin'." A recovering addict's response is "Hell yes I'm addicted and hell yes I'm gonna stay away from my poison!"

The challenge with recovering from any sort of addiction is that no one can cause you to see things in a healthy way if you are not ready to look at it all by yourself. Frequently the inner Voice tells us that our behaviors are dangerous and detrimental to our overall well-being, but we continue because it has become a habit, and habits are difficult to change. And change is very hard. Very few people are really ready to take a clear look into themselves and honestly evaluate the truth. And to complicate things further, truth is not a constant state; as we acquire new data, the truth constantly changes. So, what was our truth yesterday may not be our truth of today or tomorrow. In order to gain clarity in life, you must evaluate the situations as they stand at the moment. Sure, the pain meds helped me before. Sure, more pain meds would have probably helped me in the future, but when I was preparing to quit, the truth of my present reality was that: they are not helping me today. They were no longer serving me in any way, shape or form. I was tired of being full of toxicity and being surrounded by toxic people. When I started to end toxic relationships, the other toxic behaviors quickly followed suit. In the same seven-month period, I quit smoking, quit taking opiates and all other drugs, broke up with an entire group of friends that were not strong or appropriately supportive, put my dog of thirteen years to sleep, and observed the seven-year anniversary of my father's death. Change was surrounding me and it was inevitable that I would make these changes all on my own, while inside my own cocoon. There were no external factors influencing my decisions to create change in my life. It was simply that I had decided that I should be the one to determine if I was happy or not. Other people were simply distractions. Rather than continue to place my focus on other people and what THEY thought, I knew that seclusion would be the most effective way for me to evaluate who I was. I knew I could be more than what I was seeing, even if it meant being alone for a while. Only when we are ready to take a deep look into our souls are we able to accept and love our imperfections. Only when we are able to see and love our own imperfections as part of who we are and as part of what makes us whole, will we be able to see past them to new ways of living. If we harbor anger toward ourselves for the poor decisions we've made, we are prevented from conducting truthful evaluations to find more fruitful ways of conducting ourselves. Anger blocks us from introspection. Once we let go of the anger and begin to productively and proactively seek better alternatives while working on healthier problem solving, we are able to once again move in a forward motion. Anger is like the brakes of our cars. It stops us from going anywhere. Even if you push the gas while pushing the brake, you still remain motionless; just spinning your wheels.

As for most of the bad things that we "love", if we take a step back and start asking ourselves why over and over again, we can almost always find the core need that this "love" is satisfying. When someone stays in an abusive relationship out of "love", the cause and effect are generally consistent; the individual received a message early on that reinforced the existing belief that "you are just not good enough to deserve any better." We have these core messages that come from the pit of our souls. We then take neutral behaviors, link them to our interpretations, and watch a negative message develop. We become so accustomed to this message that we begin to only hear the things that reinforce it. It's like when you're at a party and everyone is talking and laughing. As soon as you hear someone say your name, you immediately look around. We are programmed to recognize our names, even in a noisy room. We are programmed to hear, do, and seek out that which is familiar. When someone repeats an abusive pattern, such as drugs, the cause and effect are often the SAME; the path of least resistance for that person is different from the codependent or abused. But the message is the same and the desire to be loved is the same, it just manifests itself differently.

When I was on the most medication, I could

walk into my grocery store and EVERYONE at the pharmacy would wave and say "hello". By being a legal drug addict, I had established a place for myself in the world. I was known as someone that could take a ton of pain meds and someone that had exorbitant amounts of pain. This made me someone, got me attention, and made me feel special. Now, as a recovering addict, I have the same level of notoriety from a different cause. Bottom line is that the effect is still the same. These behaviors make me feel loved in some way. So not only was my body addicted to the drug, but my head and heart were also addicted to the attention I received because of it. What a mind-fuck.

I spent some time on a pro-methadone website asking questions about people's pain and their decisions to stay on an opiate for the rest of their lives. These people saw nothing wrong with it and were actually rather angry that I, or anyone that doesn't want to be on a drug forever, would post something anti-methadone. Actually, not even anti-methadone, but rather anything that wasn't 100% pro-methadone. True, it is a pro-methadone site, but to me it seems like they should be willing to hear ALL sides. They are missing a whole piece to the puzzle and they are refusing to look for it at all.

I've read posts by addicts that have kicked heroin more than once but CANNOT stop methadone. It is a totally synthetic drug used to replace a naturally occurring plant: the poppy. Man's futile attempt at "fixing" nature. Blasphemously changing chemical properties to suit their own selfish needs...

I believe that everyone must find his/her own way. I believe that my way is right for me and might not be right for anyone else. I believe that in order to make the best decision for myself, it is important to have as much data as possible. Including other perspectives that do not agree with mine is essential to my personal evolution.

When we become frustrated and/or angry, it is because we are experiencing a conflict with our core values. However, core values become muddled unless one has a nearly obscene level of personal clarity. It is through such crystalline clarity that the truth may be revealed. If we spend our time evaluating life as it occurs, not as it once occurred or as we hope it will occur, we are able to not only stay present with ourselves, but we are also able to see things with a level of precision that is not possible any other way. With one foot either in yesterday or tomorrow, we are unable to maintain sight of today. It gets lost so easily.

Please do not misunderstand me here. I do believe that there are reasons why someone might need to stay on certain meds for an extended period of time. However, I also believe that there is a large population that uses medications/drugs as a crutch and they are simply too afraid to walk without it. It has become a comfortable habit, and most people are resistant to change. Change is difficult and requires a great deal of self-reflection and dedication. It seems, to me, that few people are willing to go through the growing pains necessary to support consistent and forever changes.

I've also heard the argument that there is a difference between being an addict and simply being dependent, and that being dependent is okay but being an addict is a problem. I looked at some general answers on some generic "question" websites (take your pick...there are a million of 'em) to see what the general population thinks and it seems that most people think: they are basically the same thing or that addiction is physical and dependency is only mental/emotional. To sum up Webster's, dependency is to "rely on for support or aid" and addiction is to "give oneself up to a strong habit". My college psych professor used them nearly interchangeably: "addictive drugs produce a biological or psychological dependence in the user." My conclusion is that the pro-drug people say that dependency is okay because it makes it easier for them to justify their behaviors. It isn't a problem, but rather something that they need to be able to function, like insulin for a diabetic. From the research I've done, I have yet to find evidence that one can manifest his own insulin by thinking it. However, one CAN manifest significant pain reduction by thinking about it. Conversely, one can increase levels of pain by thinking about it. I'm not talking about semantics. I'm talking about the fact that our minds, in all their own magnificent glory, can regulate our pain center without synthetic or naturally occurring toxins. Pain is a state of mind, a message from the body. Drug use is a mental choice. The two go hand in hand. When the decision-making process becomes controlled by the dependency, an addiction has developed.

One very significant problem for a prescription drug addict, however, is that the "professional" is enabling the addiction to continue. When a person is in mental or physical pain and he/she is receiving meds for treatment, that person will do just about anything to fix the problem. Many doctors would rather give a fix quick than deal with the cause of the issue, or perhaps find a more proactive alternative. Doctors and other "health professionals" should take into consideration that: (a) there is a mental impairment due to pain and (b) that they may be the only person a patient trusts. I can nearly guarantee that if a doctor makes a recommendation, MOST people, at least in western society, believe it will help or will believe it is the best treatment for whatever it is they are trying to correct. When my pain was at its worst, I always said that I would eat a pile of rocks if the doctor said it would take the agony away. Pain clouds our judgment. Just as I recommend that one does not rely solely on his/her own judgment when withdrawing, the same is true when pain is involved. So, since one's judgment is impaired, I would THINK that it would be the job of the medical community to aid with the judgment.

Research has shown that a person can move the level of her pain scale between a nine and a four JUST BY HER THOUGHTS! How else can we explain Buddhists monks that get into horrific accidents but experience NO pain? It's been shown through MRI and has been tested on chronic pain patients. We are, just now, starting to understand the fundamental mechanisms of pain. Since the "experts" admit to not having full comprehension of pain, is it truly safe to say that they know what they're doing? When my father was dying and I was pissed at the medical world, my mother simply said, "They are *practicing* medicine." That's all the medical community is doing: practicing. So, if we have "experts" admitting that there just might be a bit more to pain, addiction, and a hoard of other things, can't we think, even for just a second, that there might be another way, other alternatives to our "take-a-pill-and-fix-it-quick problem"? Perhaps if the pharmaceutical companies spent even a tenth of their research money on the causes of the problems and not just on a temporary fix, we might exist in a much more peaceful and harmonious society. At the very least, one with fewer addicts.

Recently my friend asked me when I

started feeling good again. As I thought about it, I realized there wasn't one day when I said, "Okay, it's all over." It was a process, where every day I noticed the discomfort less and less, until whatever was remaining had simply been assimilated into my daily routine. This is also how I describe my level of pain. The reason for me taking the meds is still with me, but I've adjusted my thinking and my way of living to accommodate it. It's no longer that I'm in pain, but rather my lower back is simply something that I treat a little bit differently than other parts of my body. I rub her, I talk to her, and I do everything I can to make her feel better, without any external assistance or substances. I believe that the power to heal lies within. If Buddhist monks can control their pain with their minds, why can't I? Why can't I walk up to the pain management doctor and say, "You're wrong. I will NOT be in pain forever and I don't need you or anyone else to stop it for me."

One thing to keep in mind is that as you break off your relationship with drugs or whatever you are withdrawing from, you will probably need to break off your relationship with some other things too. Like the people you associate drugs with, whether they are friends, family, professional, whomever. You will also need to break up with the drug addict part of yourself: the part that thinks taking diazepam to feel a little better is okay, the part that cries when you dump the drugs down the toilet, the part that wants a valium when things aren't going quite the way you want. Those are just old habits and coping mechanisms.

Once you gain sobriety, you will also need to gain new coping mechanisms. Healthy mechanisms. For example, you don't want to replace your ability to take a pill with your ability to eat an entire package of cookies. While both can provide instant gratification, there are most definitely long-term consequences. When we take drugs for any reason, pain included, we become accustomed to the "quick fix" lifestyle. We feel we deserve that instant gratification and we are able to justify it to ourselves. The problem with this behavior, however, is that it's not sustainable in regard to long-term health. B and I literally referred to heroin as "instant gratification".

There have been moments when I was feeling especially anxious and nervous and my initial thought was, "God, I wish I had some diazepam." As I started to notice this way of thinking, it occurred to me that it had been my way of thinking and coping for over 15 years. I then began to evaluate the feelings associated with nervous energy and started to dissect them and what they mean to me. I worked on understanding my body's personal coping mechanism and was able to come to a much healthier, effective, and long-term solution: When I'm tired, I drink green tea instead of taking four or five caffeine pills. When I'm sore, I walk and stretch instead of taking two or three muscle relaxers. When I can't sleep, I get up and read instead of taking two sleeping pills. Our bodies are resilient and will always take care of us if we step out harm's way. When we allow our mental functioning to try to control or alter our physical functioning, problems arise. That is why addiction is so painful. It is our mind that perpetuates the addictive cycle until our body has no choice, but to follow orders from our programmed minds. Once our body becomes addicted, it does everything it can to make us keep going. Withdrawal is not our body's way of saying, "more and more drugs please." It is our body's way of saying, "If you EVER do this to me again, I'll ensure you'll feel like living hell for months. EVERY TIME..."

I'm sure that there are a great many people in my audience that will scoff at this, but let's put it in perspective. When we are children, there is no desire for an altered state of consciousness. Being innocently aware and open to the possibilities is, quite frankly, plenty of stimulation. As we mature, however, the already-closed-off adults in our lives shut down those natural portals of enthusiasm. We, subconsciously, mimic their behavior and strive to be just like them. Since they do not wander around in a constant state of wonder and amazement, we too begin to lose that precious gift. Not lose, precisely, but rather bury it in the bullshit of our day-to-day drama. Children use their imaginations to find their own altered states of reality. They can play for hours with the simplest items and yet have the most magical day. How many adults can do that? How many adults are content enough with their own psyche to generate altered realties and new perspectives on life? Yet, children do it CONSTANTLY. Their bodies are pure and simple and are able to keep the mind safe since outside influences have not yet corrupted their thought patterns. Once these influences begin to take hold and the conscious mind takes control, the body quickly loses immediate power until it reaches a point of critical mass. The mind, then, is forced to deal with the pain and suffering. Since it is our mind that teaches us about quick fixes, it is our mind that nourishes quick fix behaviors. It's, really, quite a shitty way to exist. If we allow our bodies to heal and we learn to take care of them, we will find a much greater level of joy, comfort, and contentment in our everyday lives. It is, truly, not complicated. However, we allow the drama of others to impact the simplicity we should be striving for.

This is not to say that, as adults, we are not dealing with complicated and challenging issues. Life in this society is complicated and challenging, but the way we react to and deal with situations is all based on our perspective. Take the victim mentality. These people feel that everything is someone else's fault or responsibility. They refuse to take a clear and sincere look into themselves to determine where their responsibility lies, because they refuse to take ownership. They live a life in which they believe things just happen to them by external forces. They are unable to seek out the intrinsic thoughts, values, and behavior-drivers that may have contributed to their presently undesirable situation. They are unable to see their role in the unfolding events, so, they are unable to make progress in improving their current state of affairs. They are stuck on a treadmill that they believe someone else has not only placed them on, but is controlling the speed of. It never occurs to them to just step off because that would be taking personal responsibility and they feel they have no control; thus no blame. They believe all of the complications and challenges of life are things dropped on them and if one believes he/she is not responsible, there is simply no way he/she can create solutions. It's a never-ending cycle of martyrdom. In my experience, it seems that when someone is trapped in the world of drug abuse, they will ALWAYS believe it is external forces at work. A crappy job, a stupid car accident, unhappy marriage, because the spouse is an asshole, etc., etc., etc.. Nothing is their fault. EVER. Since self-evaluation and critique is a long and difficult process, victims often turn to the quick fix of a pill or a cocktail or a puff or a plunger. This perpetuates the negative cycle that has begun to assert full control and the person begins to feel trapped by something not of her choosing. It's really difficult to fix something that you can't see and you believe doesn't belong to you. So, the cycle continues. Poor me, have a cocktail. It's not my fault that everyone's out to get me, take a pill.

MORAL: We are never faced with adversity we cannot handle and all adversity is part of our own, special path, designed just for us.

Chapter 9

PRE-CONCLUSION

It's kind of strange to write a conclusion before I'm done with the book, but I'm hoping it will bring me some focus.

Why did I write this book? Why did I open myself up for the whole world to see? Why did I decide to stand emotionally naked on a soapbox on the street corner of Amazon books? Why? Why couldn't I let this go? Why do I get angry when someone tells me I shouldn't publish this or when someone tells me this stuff isn't true or real?

Now, I sit, trying to answer those questions...and you know what? I don't know the answer, but I'll try.

When I string all the stories of my life together, a few things are very apparent. First, many of my experiences are things that many people would not be able to survive, never mind reliving them on paper. And not only survive, but thrive as a result of. They are big. They are dramatic and they may sound fabricated. Sometimes, I barely believe these things all happened to me. I read them as if they are someone else's story and I actually find them quite entertaining. I've spent years distancing myself from the memories so that I would be able to tell them. While when I really write from the place of their creation, which is very painful, I am still able to draw a wall around my heart when I read them and imagine someone else telling me these stories. Still, they always make me so very sad. I want to hug this girl, this woman, this person, and let her know that everything's going to be okay. That she IS loved, that she IS special, and that she IS worth it.

Really, that's why I get angry. Nobody should ever feel so lost and alone and unwanted and unloved. EVER. These are horrible ways to feel, and while I do not regret any of my experiences, I regret that they continue to happen to other people everywhere. Every day it makes me hurt. It makes my heart ache. It, literally, makes me weep. Not for myself, but for the ongoing pain that others experience. I understand it and I wish it on nobody. My goal with this book is to try to show that while we all must go through excruciatingly painful trials and tribulations in life, they do not have to own us. Or break us.

I can no longer be afraid of the repercussions of trying to do this. Instead, I must fear the repercussions of doing nothing; of knowing that I could have made an impact in someone's life but instead I allowed fear of humiliation, of dredging up the horrific pain, of public ridicule and intense judgment to prevent me from taking action. The risk to me is very much outweighed by the good that this can do. This is my mission, this is my calling. My job is to show the world that you can grow up without knowing love (even if the people in your life THINK they were giving it to you), but because it truly is the magic that holds the cosmos together, it is still all around you. Always. You can never ever escape it. You just have to know how to find it. It's there. I promise. It's always been there. It is the wind that suddenly rises up to caress your tearstained cheek. It is the rain that begins to fall in rhythm to your sobs. It is the sun that rises to end the horror of your nightmares. It is the full moon, lit like a candle to light your way. It is the song on the radio that seems to be playing just for you. It is the phone call from the friend you were thinking about. It is love and it is always available to cloak and shield you from the turmoil of human emotion. It is at your disposal, hanging in your closet, waiting to be taken out and wrapped around a warm, living, breathing body. It needs to be taken out, worn, and to be shown off. It needs to feel you beneath it, like a lover awaiting the arrival of someone special. To roll together, to envelop each other, to need each other, to want each other. Love and humanity are forever bound by the eternal flow that is existence. We cannot be without love. But love will be here long after we are gone. It is the magic stardust, the face in the moon, a puppy's kiss, and the upheld arms of a baby waiting to be scooped up and snuggled. It is everything. So simple. So perfect. So real.

BUT, after spending a ton of time talking to my counselor about it, she believes (and I'm starting to) that even though "society" tells us women that we must behave in a certain way, there are still men out there that appreciate us for the way we WANT to behave, the way that's natural. I can't see myself being with someone that doesn't love and appreciate me for ALL of who I am. All the bullshit in the beginning, the wondering and doubting is all self-induced, and that's my deal. Once the relationship actually begins, however, the game changes. Feelings are real. Your perception is your reality, and the only factor that can alter that reality is more evidence. Something that HE must provide, either by conversation or by repeated behavior over time. Really, both work, but opening the lines of communication can never, ever, ever hurt matters. Even if he tells you things you don't want to hear, it will give you more data to make better decisions regarding the relationship.

As for lying to yourself, WHY would you do that? You have been protecting yourself for so long, why would your inner being suddenly stop doing that and put you in a place of intense danger? Spend some time this weekend with that inner little girl or boy of yours, and listen to his/her fears and desires. Quiet your mind and let him/her speak to you. He/she'll tell you what he/she's afraid of, and you can then take action to protect him/her. I do not believe, however, that the "real" you (id, ego, superego) will lie to you. What lies to you are those stupid, fucked-up

174

messages that we've heard from society and our childhoods. Our job as grown-ups is to crush that message and replace it with what's true... YOU, my darling, are a beautiful, amazing, gifted, incredible, ray of sunshine that brightens any room you walk into. Let yourself shine, smash those stupid old messages, and let love flow. It is, after all, the oh-so-simple key to the entire universe. If you move through life in a state of love, for yourself and for others, you will be all right. Besides, you will never, ever, ever be faced with something that you cannot handle. The Powers That Be ALWAYS make sure of that. Even when we feel like we are about to lose our fucking minds because we obsess and analyze everything to death. Fear of rejection forces us to really not be our true selves, and it limits our potential. Like I've said if I can't be intense and goofy and silly and stupid and curious and playful all in the beginning of a relationship, why on earth would I want to spend time with someone at all? I know I'm all of those things and I know that many people can't handle it, but if I'm not those things, then I'm not being me. If I don't let the love flow naturally, I'm cheating everyone involved, including myself. We often say, "if it's worked for me in the past"..., but the past is a mere prelude to the present. Each moment is merely a stepping-stone to the next, to create the path that is life. I've grown into myself more in the past five years than I ever thought I could. I'm a grown up now and

I've gotten some superglue and mended my broken heart. I'm looking for healthy people that can provide healthy messages. I'm tired of feeling like I've failed in life. I'm tired of it never being enough. I'm tired of never being good enough. I'm tired of falling. Besides, how many times can Humpty Dumpty really fall off the wall before she's broken for good? I'm 37, and I think I'm done.

Chapter 10

CONCLUSION

First, I'd like to again say that this book is in no way an attempt to simply air my dirty laundry or to point fingers or place blame regardless of what some people think. It's nothing like that. While it started as a therapeutic exercise, it turned into something that I believe may help others, somehow. I had no intention of writing a book, or at least not this book, when this whole cathartic writing thing started, but as the writing process continued, a valuable truth became evident. That truth is that it IS possible to change the messages we learn. It IS possible to become more than we think we can; to grow more than others think we can. Magic IS possible. Love IS everywhere. We CAN impact our lives and we CAN effect change. Now, I'm not afraid to stand up on a mountaintop and shout at the top of my lungs....IT IS YOUR CHOICE!!!!! We all have choices. We all have power. We all have options. Life is really nothing more than a choose-your-own-adventure storybook...and I choose to live my life in love.

APPENDIX:
Things I Learned
about Opiate Withdrawal

The Plan: breaking up is hard to do

Today is the day that I've finished the book. Well, most of it. I have a few things to add about quitting bad behaviors. And so by now you know a piece of who I am and that I'm relatively qualified to talk about this. You know that this is NOT easy, that it WILL hurt, and you may consider giving up with every miserable tug inside your legs or when the hands of the clock seem to go backwards. I am hoping that with the plan I outline, and with the encouragement I share, YOU will not go backwards. You will rise to the challenge, look this evil addiction in the face, and say, "NO MORE! If THAT girl can do it, SO CAN I!!!"

Before we get started, I must say this...
I do NOT recommend doing it the way I did. It was hard. It was dangerous and it could have killed me. BUT, if you feel you have no choice (I couldn't afford to go to a withdrawal clinic), and if you have a ROCK-SOLID support network (doctors, friends, caretaker, etc.), and above all you believe, 100%, that you CAN do it, then these are the steps I would recommend. Please remember a very obvious fact. I am not a doctor. I have never been a doctor. Nor will I ever be a

179

doctor. I'm just a recovering opiate addict. Nothing more. Nothing less.

~**First** things first. Do NOT, I repeat, do NOT try to drop your last FIVE milligrams while working!!! TAKE A WEEK OFF. You have the flu. You are sick and terribly contagious and will infect everyone if you come in. Say whatever you have to, but do not try to be tough. Do not go to work. You will regret it. This is a time when you need to be gentle with yourself and forcing yourself to fake it for forty of the most horrific hours of your life is a very bad idea. Your responsibilities are: (1) to not take any opiate, (2) to not kill anyone, and (3) to spend all of your time and energy doing what you can to make yourself well. That's it. Nothing more. If you are reading this because you are helping someone withdraw, do not set any more expectations than that. Let them be a bitch. Let them cry and scream and yell at you. Let them call you an insensitive asshole and don't hound them for it later. Just let them do whatever they need to do as long as it's safe and will not have any negative consequences, and can easily be cleaned up. They will be more appreciative of your kindness, understanding, and patience than you can possibly imagine and you will always have the satisfaction of knowing that you truly helped save a life.

~**Second**. Take care of any pressing business matters before you start to withdraw. Pay your bills. Take the dog to the vet. Fill your meds. Get your nails done. I don't fucking care what it is, just make sure you do it before you stop! Once you hit it, you won't be able to do much of anything and you won't even care that you aren't doing anything. The only thought in your head will be how badly THIS SUCKS! Your sense of responsibility becomes nearly non-existent and the things that you end up doing will most likely be so that whatever is annoying you at that moment stops. You will not be able to think ahead whatsoever. Your thoughts will vacillate wildly from one extreme to the other. So, exist knowing that all you have to do is get though the next thirty minutes...or ten minutes. Whatever works for you. If you take care of your business before you get started, you will have no reason to feel any guilt once you are all done.

~**Third**. Go to the grocery store and get your absolute most favorite things to eat. Super easy things to make. You will not want to cook. You may not want to eat, but you should, and if there is food that's easy and appealing, you will be more likely to do so. This can be anything you like, from chips to candy to soda to whatever. Just be sure to make good things available. Your appetite will probably be non-existent, but if you are taking any kind of meds to help get you through this, food is essential. Or you might just puke them back up. As an addict, you know that's never a good idea! So, try to eat something a few times a day or at least once a day.

~**Fourth**. Buy at least one big box of Imodium (and be sure to have lots of toilet paper on hand). Take as much as you need. This is NOT your body actually releasing toxins. You are simply experiencing a side effect from your dopamine receptors that are freaking out without any opiates. Stop yourself up if you can. You will be very happy you did. What will come out of you will be horrific and stinky and miserable. When you already feel like total and complete shit, you really don't need more of it coming out of you. Take the Imodium.

~**Fifth**. Make sure you have a ton of movies. You don't even have to like them or want to watch them. It is more than helpful to have some sort of auditory and visual distraction available at all times. It gives your brain the chance to think about something, anything, other than withdrawal. The Internet can be useful, but not in the early days when just existing is difficult. You will not want to sit at your laptop. You really won't want to sit anywhere. Therefore reading can be difficult and annoying too. Being confined to a chair because there's no place else to occupy yourself is just another bad idea. So lots and lots of movies in whatever room makes you feel as comfortable as possible.

~**Sixth**. Make sure you have any withdrawal-assisting medication you may need. These cannot include natural or synthetic opiates! NO OPIATES WHATSOEVER!!! They may include: muscle relaxers, anti-nausea medication, something for anxiety, anti-diarrhea medication, and something for sleep. Keep your at-home pharmacy as LOW as you can! I strongly recommend having someone there to administer your medication. If they can't be with you all day, have them leave your doses and times for the doses and take the bottles away with them. Accidental OD's are no fun and when your judgment simply does not exist, OD's are a very real possibility...

~**Seventh**. DRINK A LOT OF WATER! KEEP HYDRATED! FORCE YOURSELF! You will probably not want to put anything in your mouth and you might not feel thirsty at all, but water will help with headaches, flushing the pollutants out and will help keep your body as regulated as possible. If you can't drink, don't beat yourself up, your body will be doing enough of that. Actually, don't beat yourself up over anything during your withdrawal. Just try to drink as many fluids as you can.

~**Eighth**. Utilize your sense of smell. Make yummy tea, burn pretty candles, smell fragrant oils. The idea is to engage as many of your other senses as possible. You will not want to utilize your sense of touch, as every inch of your body will be in agony, so occupy your time by practicing your other senses. The sense of smell is one of the most powerful and can help you revert back to times of happiness.

~**Ninth**. You may sneeze. A lot. Like eight or nine times in a row, about fifteen times a day. You do not have a cold. You are not allergic to opiate withdrawal. You are not getting sick. This is normal! It is simply another dopamine side effect. DO NOT take an antihistamine. DO NOT take anything unless you absolutely have to! Keep your toxin levels as low as you can. Just let the sneezes happen. They will eventually slow in number and frequency, but only after your brain starts to regain control. Please, remember that the opiate has been running your life and you are now taking it back. If you put it in that perspective, what are a few sneezes?

~**Tenth**. Keep blankets and winter clothes on hand. You might be cold constantly. Just another dopamine effect, not to worry. Your body will slowly regain control of its thermostat, but in the meantime, bring layers wherever you go.

~**Eleventh**. Take baths or showers as often as you can. It may seem nearly impossible to muster the energy to get yourself into the tub, but you will feel instant relief. Warm water is terribly soothing to the muscles and acts as a natural relaxant. Hot water will help to clean your pores, thus allowing the toxins another escape route. Spend as much time in the water as you can.

~**Twelfth**. As soon as you possibly can, begin taking L-lysine and Folic Acid. These will help rebuild your neural pathways, which is the part of the brain that is impacted by extended opiate use. You want these fixed ASAP. Until these are repaired, you will not own your legs and the flu-ish feeling will remain, although it does dissipate a little bit each day. Same with the sneezing and the diarrhea. There is no quick fix for withdrawal. There are consequences, but the long-term benefit of existing drug-free far outweighs the discomfort. Remember, withdrawal is temporary. You have the rest of your life to feel good inside your skin!

~**Thirteenth**. Walk as much as you can and try to eat potassium rich foods. This helps alleviate a great deal of the muscle discomfort and will help pass the time.

~**Fourteenth**. Do not be afraid to ask for help. Withdrawal is difficult and it is not time to try to prove anything. There may be times when you burst into tears or scream or just need someone to tell you it's gonna be okay. The support of those that care about you, even if in a simply clinical way, can make the seemingly impossible times appear much less daunting. Another critical factor of help is: to allow someone else's judgment to take the place of your own. Your own thinking will be totally unfocused and all over the map, using someone else as your "Jiminy Cricket" can prove very useful. I spoke to my therapist at least three times per day during the first week. She would let me rant and rage and cry, all the while letting me know that she was there for me and that it would get better. She would never tell me when, but she would promise that it would not last forever. She was my voice of reason and the only voice that made sense. I used her to do my cerebral processing as often as I needed.

~**Fifteenth**. Be kind to yourself. Do not set unreasonable expectations. To be perfectly honest, while withdrawing, the only expectation should be to not take the drug of choice. Be a bitch. Be immature. Be selfish. It's all okay. Your only priority is to make it through the throes of withdrawal. The people that care about you will not hold poor behavior against you. Just be sure that you've got a few key ground-rules to adhere to. Everything else can be cleaned up after you are cleaned up. For me, my rules were: (1) get through the next thirty minutes opiate free. (2) no random sex. (3) do not kill anyone. Everything else was fixable. I had no guilt for my poor behavior or attitude because I knew that it was only temporary. It was nothing more than a result of the current situation and was not a constant state of who I am or would be once the withdrawal was over. It was temporary and fleeting and a way to protect myself from any more pain. It was nothing more than that.

~**Sixteenth**. As soon as you are clean and functioning, do a cleanse. You need to get all of that icky residue OUT of your colon and intestines so that your pipes are clean of all the yucky remnants of the opiates. My personal favorite is from **www.drnatura.com**. The website is pretty graphic, but from personal experience, I can guarantee that it works.

~**Seventeenth**. Once your body belongs to you again, you may find some level of bitterness and anger. This may be directed at the person that first got you high or the doctor that prescribed your drug of choice. This is totally normal. However, anger is generally just a way to avoid looking at the root of the problem. The root of your addiction is nothing more than you and the sum of your experiences. There is or was something going on behind the scenes that encouraged or forced your behavior to get out of control.

One way to fight back and take full ownership for what you've just experienced is to find a way to take your power back. You've already started by making the decision to get off the drugs. Once you make it through the withdrawals, you are one step closer, but once you are whole and healthy again, you may still feel a need to take action. Do not just sit on this desire! There are countless ways to spread the light that you've just been given back. This can be something as simple as putting a coin in someone's expired meter or volunteering at a soup kitchen. You can talk to a homeless person or any person experiencing some level of despair. You can pick up a lost dog or hold a crying friend's hand. Once you transition the anger to a proactive solution, the anger will dissipate immediately. You now own the emotion and the result. Anger is simply a distraction, a way for us to avoid the problem. Move past it, let it go, and start to make a positive change in your life and in the world around you. This is the only way to take the power back from the drugs and toxic people that have been in your life. Your life belongs to nobody, but you. That includes all the successes and all of the failures. Do not attempt to release ownership of your behaviors or you will never learn and grow from them.

~**Eighteenth**. Keep in mind that cleansing yourself from opiates, or any drug, is both very physical and very mental. It will be the most difficult and rewarding housecleaning you can EVER do. As a recovering addict, I can assure you that every painful second of withdrawal is even more than worth it. It's as if I was walking through life with black lenses over my eyes. Once I got through the drugs, once I started working to be the best person I can possibly be, in all areas of my life, clarity began to sweep over me in glorious waves. Grass is truly greener, roses are truly redder, and my dog's fur is truly softer. Any sort of addiction intensely dulls the life experience. It is impossible to sustain a state of constant wonder and amazement while taking something that numbs your senses, your mind, and your body.

~**Nineteenth**. After some time, you will most definitely begin to feel like your old, sunny self again. However, PAWS (post acute withdrawal syndrome) may take many weeks or even months to complete its course, but slowly you will begin to return to "normal". The primary focus of my own personal PAWS has been the lack of ownership of my legs. They had aches and discomfort for weeks. I had a difficult time sitting still and was almost always uncomfortable, but I was able to sleep through the night, which helped provide major relief. When I wasn't sleeping and the only reason I knew my legs were mine was because they happened to be attached to my hips, I was out of my mind with agony. The other thing that seemed to help the most was exercise. Walking made the aches subside, but it did become increasingly difficult during the last five milligram withdrawals to do much of anything, let alone take a walk. After about two weeks, I started to exercise...slowly. After six weeks, I started getting up at 5:30 am and working out for 45-60 minutes about five days per week.

~~~~~~

Please, please, please know that these steps are useful to rid oneself of any addiction. While getting over any toxic substance or relationship may not result in physically smelling badly, a warm shower can be very cleansing. Just replace "opiate" with whatever it is you are trying to rid yourself of. These are the steps that worked for me, and now, I'm that girl...

...And a very special thanks to:

Amanda Lampert

Amy Mackett

Andrea Lampert

Andy Schreyer

Angela Peck

Ariella

Bonnie Amman

Bre Robinson

Buddy Crayton

David Carano

Elisabeth Amman

Erin Hanzlik

Erin Howard

Frank Jimenez

Heather Findlay

Heather Kane

Jason Burke

Jeanie Robb

Jim Irving

Joel Scoles

Jon Marts

"Judge" Tom Fay

Karen Casavant

Kenny Gallagher

Kiar Brown

Lincoln Williams

Lisa Anderson

Lisa Barboza

Maggie Toews

Maria Gale

Mary Noor

Megan Anderson

Michelle Crayton

Michelle Rodriguez

Mike Foley

Pamela Valentine

Paul Haugh

Penny Rieker-Rodriguez

Susan Cannon-Barcheski

Tina Garcia

Tom Fay Jr.

Trish Brownell Hebert

Truck Santos

Victoria Wilcox

Vicky Lampert

And to my dogs Charlie Bear, Maggie, Beetle Baylee, Rudy, and Nimbus

7998806R0

Made in the USA
Charleston, SC
28 April 2011